Stupid
Windows™
Tricks

Stupid
Windows™
Tricks

Bob LeVitus
and
Ed Tittel

▲▼ **Addison-Wesley Publishing Company, Inc.**

Reading, Massachusetts ◊ Menlo Park, California ◊ New York ◊
Don Mills, Ontario ◊ Wokingham, England ◊ Amsterdam ◊ Bonn ◊
Sydney ◊ Singapore ◊ Tokyo ◊ Madrid ◊ San Juan ◊ Paris ◊ Seoul ◊
Milan ◊ Mexico City ◊ Taipei

Many of the designations used by manufacturers and sellers to distinguish their products are claimed as trademarks. Where those designations appear in this book and Addison-Wesley was aware of a trademark claim, the designations have been printed in initial capital letters (for example, "Windows" for Microsoft Windows).

ISBN 0–201–60840–5
ISBN 0–201–58144–2

Sponsoring Editor: David Rogelberg
Project Editor: Joanne Clapp Fullagar
Technical Reviewers: Brian Moura and Enrique LaRoche
Cover design by Ronn Campisi
Set in 11-point Bitstream *Latin 725* by Bob LeVitus

1 2 3 4 5 6 7 8 9 – MW – 9695949392

First printing, March 1992

This book is dedicated to three different groups of stellar individuals, all of whom contributed in one way or another: first and foremost, to the intrepid programmers whose work made this book possible; second, to the wild and crazy dudes at Microsoft who made the whole Windows phenomenon possible; and last (but definitely not least) to my family: Suzy, Austin, Chelsea, and Dusty, without whose support and helpful uptake on some much-needed slack I never could have finished working on this book.

E.T.

I couldn't agree more. First and foremost, to the programmers who developed the tricks—thank you, thank you, thank you, thank you. You are the true heroes of the Stupid series of books. And to the Windows development dudes and dudettes—thanks for making the GUI safe for mere mortals. Finally, to my family—Lisa, Allison, Max, and Sadie—I love you guys.

B.L.

Acknowledgments

I'd like to continue to thank Jamie Sanders, former chief CompuServe Sys*Op for Novell, Inc. (alas, he got too good at his job and has now been kicked upstairs), who got me both interested and completely hooked on the whimsies and wonders of online communication.

I'd also like to thank three other Windows stars who helped me along the way: Brian Moura, the reigning king of Windows resources, who knows more about Windows than anybody else I have ever met and has bailed me out of more than a few tight spots; and Eric Robishaw, the manager of Software Exchange, who helped me over a few last-minute bumps on the hardware road to Windows nirvana; and Enrique LaRoche, technical reviewer and beta tester supreme.

To the readers of our first PC-based book—*Stupid PC Tricks*—thanks for the mail, the bug and problem reports, and the helpful suggestions about how to make things work better. I have tried to incorporate many of your suggestions for improving the installation and use of the tricks into this book.

My most fervent thanks are reserved for Bob LeVitus, who was kind enough to invite me to continue the saga we started so successfully with *Stupid PC Tricks* here in *Stupid Windows Tricks*. This is getting to be so much fun, I can't believe that it's work! Apparently, stupidity is a limitless resource, with an endless capacity to amuse.

E.T.

What he says goes double for me.

The only thing I have to add are special thanks to the gang at Addison-Wesley for taking a chance on Stupid in the first place, and for keeping the faith through four stupid projects.

Oh, and extra-special thanks to Ed Tittel, who outdid himself this time. You are truly awesome!

B.L.

Table of Contents

Preface

Welcome to *Stupid Windows Tricks*, an outstandingly nonfunctional collection of freeware and shareware games, gadgets, and software oddities. This package contains 17 different programs, representing almost 1,655K of what we hope is pure fun and harmless entertainment. We know you'll have as much fun playing with it as we had putting it together.

Many of the tricks are shareware. If you're not familiar with the term, shareware is a wonderful form of low-cost software marketing. Essentially, it is try-before-you-buy software that you can copy and distribute, but it is usually subject to some restrictions. In most cases, shareware authors will encourage you to give copies to friends to try. But when you find yourself using a particular piece of shareware long enough to call that use habitual or regular, you are asked to send the author a few dollars—from $2 to $25 each for the shareware tricks in this book.

Unless you have access to a large collection of shareware, there is always some cost associated with obtaining those shareware programs you want to try out. You could use a modem and download them from a local bulletin board (BBS) or an online service such as CompuServe, America Online, or GEnie for between $5 and $12.50 an hour. Most user groups sell them on disks. There are even vendors who specialize in distributing shareware from whom you can also buy such disks, typically for $2 to $3 apiece.

All things considered, you could probably find all these tricks somewhere else. For any given item, you might even save a dollar or two. And, since it's perfectly legal to give your friends copies of shareware programs—even the ones in this book—you might be wondering if this book is worth $20. In response, we have to state a resounding "Yes!"

What makes it worth it? The primary reason is that we've filtered out all the rejects or also-rans. We torture-tested more than two hundred Windows tricks—a lot of them horrible—before deciding on the 17 included here. This took an enormous amount of time— time you will avoid wasting. We also spent months corresponding electronically via modem with shareware fanatics, asking which tricks were *their* favorites. The resulting collection contains only great tricks—the most popular ones we could find (or worst of the worst, depending on your point of view). Plus, we give you illus- trated documentation with hints, strategies, and techniques for getting the best use out of each program.

So we think you'll find this book a good value. For less than $1.25 each, which is less than what it would cost to download many of the tricks from one of the online services, you'll get to try all 17 of the tricks, complete with printed documentation.

Please remember: Buying this book does not absolve you of your responsibility to pay the authors for the shareware tricks you like. If you do like a shareware trick and use it regularly, you're honor- bound to pay for it. The prices the authors typically ask—$5, $8, or $10—are pretty reasonable, considering what their commercial equivalents cost. We sincerely hope you'll do the right thing.

One last word of caution: If you decide to play tricks on others, be responsible about it. Don't just change somebody else's machine and walk away. If you stick around, you'll not only get to see what happens, but you'll also be able to get them back to work with a minimal amount of downtime. Just think about how you would feel if somebody did it to you. And if you do elect to play tricks on others, remember that turnabout is fair play. If you do trick irresponsibly at the office, the job you lose may be your own!

Now, check out those tricks!

Bob LeVitus
Ed Tittel
Winter 1991

PS: Tell us what you think of *Stupid Windows Tricks*. Bob LeVitus can be reached electronically on CompuServe (76004,2076), America Online (LeVitus), and GEnie (R.LeVitus). Ed Tittel can be reached on CompuServe (76376,606), via MHS (etittel @ Novell), and on the Internet (76376.606@compuserve.com). Or, if you don't have a modem, write us care of our publisher: Addison-Wesley Publishing Company, Trade Computer Books, 1 Jacob Way, Reading, MA 01867.

Introduction

Welcome to Stupid Windows Tricks

Chances are good that you're already using Microsoft Windows if you're buying this book. *Stupid Windows Tricks* (SWT) is a collection of some wacky and wonderful freeware and shareware for the Windows environment, with a pronounced emphasis on fun over utility.

If this is your first foray into Windows, we strongly recommend that you investigate one or more of the resources described in Appendix A before getting started with this book. Forewarned is forearmed: Do not tread blithely into Windows without a little help from those who've gone before you! Another way to look at this is as a chance to learn from the experience—and mistakes—of others.

As you read the book, you'll find us throwing around all kinds of exotic technical terminology. Please don't be disheartened—we've tried to corral all the jargon into our glossary at the back of the book and to supply definitions for all such esoterica in as everyday English as the topics will allow. Feel free to consult the glossary or any of the other references if something isn't familiar or doesn't make sense. Also, please send us your comments if things don't clear up with a little effort.

System Requirements

Ostensibly, Windows will run on any IBM PC or compatible platform. Windows runs in three different operating modes, each based on a particular family of IBM PCs or compatible machines, that span the entire family of IBM PCs:

- Real mode, intended for use on the original IBM PC or PC/XT platform. These machines incorporate Intel's 8088 or 8086 microprocessors and are purely single-tasking, and limited to a maximum of one megabyte (1MB) of Random-Access Memory (RAM). By today's standards, these 8-bit machines are old and slow, and Windows behaves accordingly. Windows will run in Real mode on these machines, but it won't be very fast, nor will you have much room for running multiple programs or working with multiple tricks at the same time. Higher-powered machines can use Real mode to run older versions of Windows software (including some of the tricks) by invoking the program in Real mode using the /r switch on the command line, but they will be hampered by memory limitations.

  Microsoft recommends that these machines have a full 640 Kilobytes (K) of RAM installed with a color display (CGA or EGA) and a mouse to get the best use of Windows in Real mode.

  One very important change that takes effect with Microsoft's introduction of Windows 3.1 is the elimination of Real mode support. Among other things, this means that 8088- or 8086-based PCs (that is, , the original PC and PC/XT and compatibles) will not be able to run Windows 3.1; it also means that applications written for versions of Windows prior to 2.0 will not work in the 3.1 environment.

  Because an 80386SX PC will run both standard and enhanced mode Windows applications and because such a machine costs very little more than an 80286 PC, we strongly recommend that anyone considering an upgrade from one of the older platforms about to be left behind by Windows make the jump all the way to an 80386SX.

- Standard mode, intended for use on the PC/AT or compatible platforms. Standard mode is written to exploit the power of the Intel 80286 microprocessor. The 80286 is a 16-bit microprocessor that can perform a brain-damaged kind of multitasking and can also address up to 16MB of RAM.

  By today's standards, a 286-based PC is a no-frills workhorse machine. It is in use in homes and offices around the world but is definitely in the Volkswagen Beetle or Ford Escort class. Windows actually works fairly well in Standard mode, but it is still kind of slow and remains limited in its ability to multitask. As the name implies, Microsoft intended that Standard mode be the basic mode for Windows operation, so higher-powered machines can run Windows in Standard mode by using the /s qualifier when invoking the program.

  Microsoft requires that a Standard mode machine be equipped with at least 1MB of RAM, more in the form of a memory expansion card if possible (2MB total RAM is recommended), a color monitor and a video display card capable of VGA or higher resolutions, and, of course, a mouse or other pointing device.

- Enhanced mode, built to take advantage of the Intel 80386 and higher-numbered microprocessors in that family (that is, the 80486), takes advantage of these processors' built-in multitasking capabilities, 32-bit horsepower, and ability to address up to 4 gigabytes (GB) of RAM to squeeze the most performance out of Windows. Even so, it can still seem slow to those who haven't learned what is worth waiting for.

In addition to being able to address large amounts of RAM when used in enhanced mode, Windows can also make use of something called virtual memory to extend its ability to accommodate programs. Virtual memory essentially turns a section of a hard disk into an extra storage area for programs, where idle programs or pieces of programs can be kept for relatively quick access when not in immediate use. The net result from this capability is that a user running Windows in enhanced mode on a machine with 4 MB of RAM can set up a runtime environment larger than 4 MB: As long as you're willing to suffer the consequences of disk-swapping—where information gets copied from RAM to disk for an outgoing program, and from disk to RAM for an incoming one—this technique can increase the size of your workspace dramatically.

Despite enhanced mode's increased capabilities relative to standard mode, it is not always the best choice for users, even those whose CPUs will support it. Even though enhanced mode permits multiple DOS applications to operate concurrently and also supports virtual memory, in many cases enhanced mode runs somewhat slower than standard mode. This is due to the overhead that use of advanced features can impose, particularly on 80386SX or lower-powered 80386 CPUs. The best rule of thumb is experiment with your mode of operation, and pick the one that works best for your typical working environment.

Microsoft recommends that an Enhanced mode machine be equipped with at least 2MB of RAM (our experience shows that 4MB is a more realistic lower limit), with color VGA or SVGA and mouse, where use of a memory management program like Microsoft's HIMEM.SYS or EMM386.EXE is also strongly encouraged.

EMM386 is an expanded memory emulator included with Windows 3.0 and with DOS 5.0—that is, it uses extended memory to emulate expanded memory. HIMEM.SYS is a memory manager included with DOS 5.0 that manages extended memory. Extended memory typically refers to RAM installed on the motherboard over the one MB Upper Memory Boundary, whereas expanded memory is memory that can be mapped anywhere above the one MB boundary through one or more page frames that switch information from upper memory over one MB into the 640K range, using one or more 16 KB regions in the upper memory region from 640K to the one MB boundary.

Expanded memory is important only to applications that are explicitly written to take advantage of it (for example, Lotus 1-2-3), but is otherwise not needed. EMM386.EXE is necessary only if you use expanded memory applications, either in Windows Real mode, or in DOS outside the Windows environment. In fact, many experts recommend that EMM386.EXE be installed on machines where Windows will be run primarily with the NOEMS switch turned on. For more information on these subjects, we encourage you to read further in the DOS and Windows manuals, and in the resources mentioned in Appendix A, *Windows Resources,* included at the end of this book.

Any of the Windows modes will do just for running the Windows tricks, but in researching the book and learning to live with Windows, we have come to endorse a common recommendation in the computing industry: If you want to run Windows, do so on a platform that supports Enhanced mode. That is where you'll be able to use Windows to its best advantage and capabilities, and where you'll get reasonably tolerable performance for everyday use. Remember, if you have to run in Real mode (or want to because of some older Windows software you need to run), you cannot use Windows 3.1: It no longer supports Real mode operation.

We follow the lead of most computer industry figures—like the columnists who write for publications like *InfoWorld* or *PC Week*—in recommending a 386SX machine as the minimum platform for enjoyable Windows use, with at least 4MB of RAM, at least a 40MB hard drive, a VGA display with on-board VRAM for better performance, and, of course, a mouse. What you decide to use is up to you, but unanimity within the trade press is rare enough that you should wonder why this is one recommendation that pretty much everybody gets behind.

One last note: Many, if not most, of the tricks in the book are written specifically for Windows 3.0. Unfortunately, Windows is not forward-compatible, so if you're running an earlier version of Windows, you will not be able to use much of the software in this book. On the other hand, Windows 3.0 is a great improvement over its predecessors, especially in terms of robustness and speed. If you haven't already upgraded, it's probably a good idea to do so. Because Windows is backward-compatible, you will be able to run software from earlier versions under 3.0 (but you may have to run in Real or Enhanced mode to keep older software working reliably).

We've constructed the disk full of tricks so that they can only be run on a PC with a hard drive. Because the Windows environment requires about 6MB to 8MB of disk space just for its own installation, we assume that anyone running Windows is doing so from a hard drive (Microsoft also makes this assumption). The installation instructions and batch files are written only for machines with hard disks. If you can make Windows run on a floppy-only system, getting access to the tricks from a floppy should be no challenge!

The Test Environment

Our own test machines included five different kinds of PCs, which we used to download and try out the original tricks. We then tested the STUP-WIN.EXE file and the tools included along with it to make sure that all of the tricks worked OK.

We then distributed the "golden" release file of our tricks to a dedicated bunch of beta testers for further review (on a slew of additional machines). Throughout the entire process, we made sure that everything worked as expected.

We can't guarantee that our tricks will work on your PC, nor can we safeguard you from harm. Hopefully, the array of machines, CPU types, and operating system versions will prove encouraging—chances are that most, if not all, of the tricks will work for you (as long as you follow the installation instructions).

Here's what we used to test the Stupid Windows Tricks:

Machine 1: A hybrid 386SX

- 16-MHz 80386SX Magitronics motherboard; AMI BIOS
- 5MB RAM
- 128MB Seagate IDE hard drive
- MS-DOS 3.31, Windows 3.0
- Samsung CJ4681 VGA display, CompuAdd 16-bit VGA card
- Microsoft Bus mouse

Machine 2: Compaq Portable 386/20

- 20-MHz 80386DX, Compaq BIOS
- 3MB RAM
- 100MB Connor IDE hard disk, integrated IDE controller
- Compaq PC-DOS 3.31, Windows 3.0
- Gas-plasma CGA display
- Logitech Serial mouse

Machine 3: Compaq Portable II

- 8-MHz 80286, Compaq BIOS
- 640K RAM
- 20MB MFM hard disk, Compaq integrated controller
- Compaq PC-DOS 3.31, Windows 3.0

- Monochrome EGA display
- Logitech Serial mouse

Machine 4: Dolch Portable 386SX Lunchbox

- 16-MHz 80386SX, Dolch/Phoenix BIOS
- 4MB RAM
- 128MB Connor IDE hard drive
- MS-DOS 3.31, 4.01, 5.0; Windows 3.0
- Monochrome LCD VGA display
- Microsoft Bus mouse

Machine 5: SoftWare Exchange 486 Mini-tower

- 33-MHz 80486, AMI BIOS
- 16MB RAM
- 128MB Seagate IDE hard drive
- MS-DOS 4.01, 5.0; Windows 3.0, 3.1ß1, 3.1ß2
- CTX Multiscan SVGA monitor, ATI Graphics Ultra card
- ATI integrated mouse

Following the industry recommendations for a 386SX platform, Machine 1 was our primary test machine. We used it first to try out all candidate tricks and then to select the final contestants. We used the current shipping version of Windows—3.0—as the primary testing and selection environment.

Machine 5 was the primary research machine and the platform on which we ran the tricks against two beta-test versions of Microsoft's next planned Windows release, tentatively named Windows 3.1. By the time you read this, Microsoft will probably be shipping that release; it should be encouraging to note that all of the tricks appeared well-behaved in that environment and should be able to coexist with the new Windows version (see installation and use instructions for specifics on individual tricks in the following chapters).

Installation Guide

The files on the floppy are structured so that you can unpack them to run on a hard disk. As stored on the original 3.5-inch floppy, these files consume almost the entire capacity of the 720K diskette. Uncompressed, these total nearly 1,655K (actually, 1,694,800 bytes or so) of information.

The only step in the installation process is to run from DOS the batch file named SWT-INST.BAT on the diskette included with the book. If you examine the contents of that diskette with the DOS DIR (directory) command, you'll see that it contains a compressed file named STUP-WIN.EXE and an uncompressed file, SWT-INST.BAT, which you will use to handle copying and decompressing the tricks files into a set of directories, one for each trick or group of tricks.

(Note: If you're already running Windows, you will either have to exit to DOS in order to run the installation program, or run it from the DOS prompt program included in the Main program group under Windows.)

The installation process is described in detail in the Installation Guide, including what you have to do at your PC's keyboard (in boldface), along with explanatory text to describe what's going on. To begin the process, you'll need to switch over to the floppy drive where you've inserted the diskette that came with the book (the following example assumes that it's in the A: drive; if not, use the appropriate drive letter):

C:\> **A:**

Assuming that you want to install the tricks on the C: drive in the WINDOWS directory, simply enter the name of the batch file at the system prompt. This will copy the compressed file to C:\WINDOWS, unpack it, and set up the directories where the tricks or groups of tricks will reside. That's it. Now you're ready to continue with each trick covered in the following chapters. For the record, here's what that command looks like:

A:\> **SWT-INST**

If you want to supply a different drive letter or a directory named something other than \WINDOWS as the base directory for the tricks, invoke SWT-INST with a drive letter and a directory path, as follows:

A:\> SWT-INST B WINDOWS\UTILS\SWT

The B indicates that you want the files copied to your B: drive and that the path into which they will be copied will be named B:\WINDOWS\UTILS\SWT.

Installing the Tricks: A Step-by-Step Guide

1. **A:**
Insert the SWT floppy into the A: drive before entering this (so the drive will have something in it when you change the drive designation to it and when you fire off the installation batch file in the next step).

2. A:\>**SWT-INST [drive] [directory]**
This runs the installation program, which copies the files to the drive specified by the first argument and the directory specified by the second argument. Both of these arguments are optional, where **drive** defaults to C: and **directory** to \WINDOWS. The installation program cleans up after itself, leaving your hard drive with the tricks in place. See Appendix B for the gory details.

When looking at a trick for the first time, if the book indicates that there's a documentation file of some kind, it's probably a good idea to read it before proceeding with the installation. While we've tried to cover all of the essential points about each trick in its own section or its own individual chapter, it's always a good idea to consult the original author's tips and information before installing a trick and using it for the first time.

You can usually recognize a documentation file by its file extension. Here are the extensions used in the various documentation files included with the SWTs in the book:

- .DOC is usually an ASCII text file. You can read this in DOS with any ASCII text editor (for example, EDLIN or EDIT) or in Windows with the Notepad.

- .TXT is usually an ASCII text file. You can read this in DOS with any ASCII text editor (for example, EDLIN or EDIT) or in Windows with the Notepad.

- .WRI indicates that this is a Microsoft Write file and must be read using the Windows Write application (which is found in the Accessories program group provided with Windows).

Squeezing the Most Out of the SWT Disk

And now a word about our special compression technology: The tricks are being distributed in a .ZIP format, using Phil Katz's PKZIP program to do the compression, and his ZIP2EXE program to turn the compressed file into a self-unpacking program. PKZIP and ZIP2EXE are two items in a very useful set of compression, decompression, and file management utilities available from PKWARE, Inc., that are in very wide use among the entire PC community (they're extremely handy for archiving lots of data on a single diskette or for compressing files before sending them somewhere by modem).

We can't recommend these utilities highly enough, so if you're interested in obtaining a copy, send $47 to PKWARE, Inc., 7545 North Port Washington Rd., Glendale, WI 53217 ($25 will suffice to register your copy if you already have one and don't want them to send you an official version with diskettes and manuals).

Disclaimer

The authors make no claims about the performance of the tricks on the Stupid Windows Tricks disk. We've tested each one on a variety of different PCs, and they all appear to work as advertised in the far-from-exhaustive testing that we did do. We feel pretty sure that none of the tricks will do any damage to your PC (like trash the hard disk or burn up the motherboard). However, we can make no guarantees—use them at your own risk.

Some tricks may conflict with other Windows programs or TSRs accessed through Windows that you normally use (a TSR is a special kind of DOS program, called terminate-and-stay-resident, that is always available at any time with a special keystroke). Some of the tricks conflict with each other; where this occurs, we try to document it.

Unfortunately, there was no way that we could test every possible combination of Windows programs, tricks, and TSRs. We sincerely apologize if something doesn't work or doesn't get along well with your current setup, but we cannot be held responsible. All we can say is, try them and see.

We both firmly believe in regular hard disk backups, and we strongly recommend that you create a fresh backup before trying any of these tricks on yourself or some unsuspecting co-worker. If you don't have a backup and things go wrong, you'll have no one to blame but yourself.

Our talented group of beta testers also alerted us to another potential source of trouble. It's particularly important to be careful about using lots of background tricks when running in a networked PC environment. Since most network drivers are themselves TSRs, it's undesirable to run background tricks in this kind of environment unless you're an experienced DOS and Windows user and can deal with the loss of your networked connection. Because network drivers and related TSRs already can consume significant amounts of RAM, adding more overhead to your system will also only diminish the usability of the remaining memory space. We repeat: If you're running on a network, avoid the background tricks that stay active all the time in our book (like the screen blankers or WinRoach) unless you're able and willing to troubleshoot possible difficulties that may result.

Avoiding Trouble

Any time you change your DOS or Windows environment—especially when you're installing a trick that runs continuously as a background task, it's wise to take a few precautionary steps to avoid conflicts or more serious potential problems.

To begin with, whenever you change anything, it's a good idea to have a backup of what you started from so you can return to a known working state easily. We recommend that you make regular backups of your entire PC environment in any case—when you're installing or running anything new, start by making a fresh backup. That way, if anything goes awry, you can get back to a pristine state easily.

This also means that it's a good idea to make a bootable floppy that contains your current system directory, along with the two important DOS files that control how your machine behaves when you start it up: CONFIG.SYS, which manages your system configuration, and AUTOEXEC.BAT, which is executed every time you start up your PC (you'll also want to include any other files with the extension .SYS, since these are typically needed to establish whatever working environment you've built for yourself). You'll also want to make copies of your initialization files (WIN.INI, SYSTEM.INI, and so on) to make sure that you can get back to where you started within the Windows environment.

This floppy will prove invaluable should any problems show up, since you can start your machine using its contents to create a known working environment from which to run your backup software (or from which you can back out changes to your working environment by hand). This can also provide a quick fix for your operating environment and may obviate having to do a complete restore from your backup.

What to Do If Your System Crashes

We certainly don't expect that any of the Stupid Windows Tricks will cause your system to crash, but in the unlikely event that some interaction between your previous environment and one or more of the tricks causes your machine to hang up or become otherwise inoperable, remember not to panic.

13

To get yourself going again, first try to reboot your PC by entering the reboot key combination: Ctrl-Alt-Delete (this is known among computer aficionados as the "three-fingered salute"). If that doesn't work, turn the machine off, wait at least 30 seconds (or until you hear the hard disk quiet down), and then turn it back on again. In most cases, the PC will run without further problems, and you'll have to decide whether or not you want to figure out what was causing the problem and whether or not you really want to use the trick that caused the problem to appear.

If the PC still won't reboot properly, restart it from your backup system floppy and remove the trick that was just installed from your Windows environment. (Remember, this may require editing WIN.INI. WIN.INI is a pure text file, and may be edited with NotePad within Windows, or with any ASCII-based text editor—like EDLIN—from DOS. Examining the file will show a number of sections including items to be loaded upon startup [LOAD= section], programs to be run automatically [RUN= section], and a great many additional sections for Windows own operation and for operation of other Windows-based programs. Please consult the Windows manual for more information about how to handle the WIN.INI file.) Again, you'll have to decide whether or not you want to figure out what's causing the problem or whether it's easier not to use the trick.

If you do decide to analyze the situation, here's what you'll have to do: Remove all of your nonstandard program groups (and any tricks you might have installed) and any non-Windows program managers or shell equivalents. Then install the trick and start installing the other components of your working environment one at a time. As each one is added, test your environment for problems. In most cases, when you add the offending program or shell, it will make itself known. This is a time-consuming and painstaking process, but it will permit you to catch the culprit(s) involved.

Eyes on Windows

   EyeCon, Eyes for Windows, and Neko

This chapter includes three SWTs that follow the cursor around as it moves across the screen: Two of them use the visual metaphor of a pair of eyes that track the cursor and the third is a small window with a playful kitten inside that also tracks the cursor. Curiously, all three of these tricks have their origins in the X-Windows world of UNIX, where Neko and the pair of eyeballs have been fixtures of stupidity for years.

Despite their apparent lack of utility, we did find one surprisingly useful application for any or all of these tricks: On an LCD screen, the cursor does not typically track very well, especially when the mouse is in motion; using any of the tricks gives a very useful visual clue about where the cursor is on the screen, even if it can't be seen at some particular moment.

 # EyeCon

What EyeCon Does

With a truly awful pun, EyeCon announces what it is: an icon that resembles a pair of eyeballs that tracks the cursor around. It is a venerable old SWT, originally written for an earlier version of Windows and rewritten for Windows 3.0.

EyeCon is a pretty faithful reproduction of the eyeballs you'll find in the UNIX X-Windows world. Like its progenitor, it's a little homely and clunky in appearance, but it does do its admittedly small job reasonably well. Unlike its progenitor, it's smart enough to blink and even to fall asleep after a period of inactivity. EyeCon also imposes minimal overhead in your Windows environment—when running, EyeCon consumes a modest 5K or so of RAM.

How to Use EyeCon

Running EyeCon is the essence of simplicity: Use the File Manager to get into the \EYES subdirectory created by the SWT install program and double-click on the file named EYECON.EXE (or use the File Manager's Run command). This will bring up the icon depicted in Figure 1. To include EyeCon as a regular part of your Windows environment, add the line:

C:\WINDOWS\EYES\EYECON

to the Run= section of your WIN.INI file. This will cause it to be loaded when Windows starts up on your computer. To change the sleep interval, create a section at the end of your WIN.INI file as follows:

**[EyeCon]
Timer=<n>**

where <n> is a whole number. This tells EyeCon to wait *n* seconds before closing one eye and another *n* seconds before closing both eyes (going to sleep).

16

Figure 1: EyeCon icon

Escaping EyeCon

To remove EyeCon from your desktop, click on the icon and close the program or use Ctrl-Esc to call up the Task List and click on End Task to stop the program. This will be a generally useful technique for stopping any of the SWTs in this book, so we'll depict it here in Figure 2.

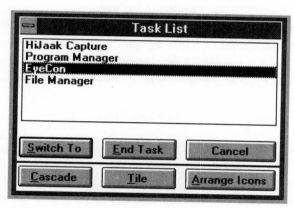

Figure 2: Use the Task List to stop SWTs

EyeCon: The Fine Print

EyeCon is the work of Nobuya Higashiyama and is offered to the public as freeware. You may copy and distribute EyeCon to anyone you choose, as long as the files EYECON.EXE and EYECON.DOC are included with each copy and no charge greater than $5 is levied for any copy. Those who wish to contact the author with bug reports, comments, or suggestions can reach him as follows:

17

Eastern Mountain Software
P.O. Box 20178
Columbus, OH 43220
Phone:(614) 798-0910
CompuServe ID: 71570,533
Internet: mead!nxh@uccba.uc.edu
UUCP: ...!uucba!mead!nxh

Author's Comments

EyeCon was written as a simple exercise in Windows programming. I'm both surprised and gratified by the responses it has generated from Windows users everywhere. Thanks to many folks who sent in comments, bug reports, and suggestions!

Also available from Eastern Mountain Software:

WinPost—Reminder Notes Manager for Windows

Use WinPost to get rid of your Post-it™ notes! This Windows utility allows the user to create and manage reminder notes. Icon Tool Bar, mouse shortcuts, and accelerator keys make this a very intuitive and easy-to-use utility. Major features include print facility, search facility, alarm notes, numerous configuration parameters, auto save, and more. Available from ASP shareware vendors, CompuServe, GEnie, and major BBSs.

EyeCon: The Files

EYECON.DOC	ASCII text file describing EyeCon program and conditions for use
EYECON.EXE	EyeCon program file

18

Eyes for Windows

What Eyes for Windows Does

For those who don't like their eyeballs boxed in, we've also included Chris Eisnaugle's more sophisticated eyeballs for your perusal. Although the name of the files that make up his work are EYES.EXE and EYES.TXT, the program icon for his interpretation of eyeball ecstasy gets labelled Ralph II by default at start-up. Figure 3 introduces Ralph's wonderful self.

Figure 3: Eyes for Windows (Ralph II), gazing heavenward

Compared to EyeCon, Ralph is a bit more advanced: His eyes are a charming blue—if you have a color monitor, that is. He blinks from time to time and will cast a wink at you whenever his icon is moved around the desktop. Unlike EyeCon, you can't make Ralph cross his eyes by placing the cursor right between them: Any time the cursor is inside the Ralph II icon, he looks straight ahead in a dignified manner. Ralph will fall asleep, however, if the mouse stays idle for more than a minute. Even though Ralph is more sophisticated, we prefer EyeCon because of the crossed eyes—we figure that if somebody stuck a cursor on the bridge of your nose, you'd cross your eyes too!

How to Use Eyes for Windows

Installing Eyes for Windows is just like installing EyeCon: From the File Manager double-click on the file named EYES.EXE (or use the Run command). The same tip about installing Eyes for Windows as a regular part of your Windows environment holds here too. Simply edit the Run= statement of your WIN.INI file to include

19

C:\WINDOWS\EYES\EYES

and Ralph will gaze longingly at your cursor every time you get into the Windows environment. If you want to give Ralph a different name, you can add a new section to your WIN.INI file as follows to provide it:

[EYES]
Name=Eye!Eye!Eye!

This name gives us a chance to top the pun used for EyeCon—it should be pronounced Ai!Ai!Ai!(whew!).

Escaping Eyes for Windows

To halt Eyes for Windows, double-click on the desktop or enter Ctrl-Esc to call up the Task List, highlight the Ralph II task name (or whatever you've renamed the program to be in WIN.INI), and click on the End Task button. Short of closing Windows, this is the only way to stop the program.

While Eyes for Windows is larger than EyeCon (25K instead of 5K), it is still modest enough to be made a regular feature of your desktop without consuming too many resources.

Eyes for Windows: The Fine Print

Like EyeCon, Eyes for Windows is also freeware and may be passed along to anyone you choose. The author can be reached at:
Chris Eisnaugle
19 Bond Street
Bridgewater, NJ 08807
Phone: (908) 685-2659
CompuServe: 76166,1257.

The author's comments provide the credits admirably, so here goes.

Author's Comments

Eyes for Windows by Chris Eisnaugle

Eyes for Windows was inspired by the eyes program found on most X-Window systems. Unfortunately, these programs lacked a personality. So I decided to update the original idea by adding more human qualities, such as blinking, winking, and falling asleep. I felt these offered a more robust and enjoyable overall application. Enjoy!

Eyes for Windows: The Files

EYES.EXE	Eyes for Windows program
EYES.TXT	ASCII text file describing program, conditions for use, and so on

 # NEKO

What Neko Does

In many ways, Neko is similar to the eyeball programs, which is why we've included it in this chapter. Since it animates a kitten in a window (*neko* is Japanese for cat), rather than a pair of eyeballs, Neko is considerably more diverting than the other programs. This is both a blessing because of Neko's enhanced entertainment value and a curse because of its higher degree of distraction. You'll have to decide what kind of cursor tracker works best for you, but there's no disputing that Neko offers a greater variety of motion and actions than the others.

The animated figure is a kitten, and in keeping with that flighty race of creatures, Neko adds scratching (both himself and the window frame), sleeping, sitting, and jumping to his relentless pursuit of the cursor. Figure 4 shows what Neko looks like running around in his window.

Figure 4: Neko at work or play

How to Use Neko

As Windows programs go, Neko is more sophisticated than the eyeball programs. It includes a control panel, depicted in Figure 5. It also behaves more like a full-fledged Windows program, which is what we'd expect from something that runs inside a real window instead of being just an animated icon like EyeCon and Eyes for Windows.

```
                    Neko Settings

  Time ( milliseconds )
  _____

  How often Neko is           125
  updated (Default 125).


     SPEED ( pixels )
     _____

  Maximum distance
  Neko can travel at          16
  one time (Default 16).


     IDLE ( pixels )
     _____

  Neko's sensitivity to
  mouse movement              6
  when idle (Default 6).


          OK              CANCEL
```

Figure 5: Neko's controls

The control panel permits you to alter Neko's update time, speed of pursuit, and sensitivity to mouse movements when idle. A little experimentation convinced us that the defaults work fine, but feel free to play with the controls if you're so inclined. Note that with Neko's greater sophistication also comes a higher demand for RAM: The program consumes about 45K of RAM, which can be worth recovering when memory space gets tight on your desktop.

Installing Neko involves either double-clicking through the File Manager or using the Run command, as with the other two programs. It can be halted either through the Task List or by closing the program through its own window controls. Neko can also be minimized to icon format by selecting Minimize through its window controls, making it quiescent (and saving some memory).

Neko also offers color controls, for both himself and for the background of his window. While playing with the settings is fun, we quickly reverted to the defaults (white cat on white background) because they were less distracting than most of the other available choices. The color controls are easily accessible from Neko's menu bar.

Escaping Neko

Unlike cats in real life, Neko is easy to get rid of: You can close the program through the control button, select Quit from the menu bar, or use the Task List to end Neko. Whichever method you choose, you'll find Neko very tractable—we preferred the Quit menu item because it was a one-click operation. But if you're busy in another application and can't see the Neko icon—and if you need to free up the RAM or CPU cycles Neko consumes—the other methods of elimination work just fine.

Neko: The Fine Print

Neko is copyrighted freeware written by Dara T. Khani, modeled after the X-Windows program of the same name. Neko may be freely distributed, providing that the text and .INI files always accompany the program. The author can be reached at the following address or on Internet: dara-khani@orl.mmc.com.

If you like Neko, please send Dara a postcard of your city. Furthermore if you would like to receive the upcoming version of Neko ("Neko runs free"), please send $5 to:

Dara T. Khani
1088 McKinnon Avenue
Oviedo, FL 32765

Author's Comments

The Windows version of Neko is written by Dara T. Khani. The original version was written by Masayuki Koba for the Macintosh. Feel free to share Neko with your friends.

Neko: The Files

NEKO.EXE	Neko program file
NEKO.INI	Neko settings file (used to edit WIN.INI)
NEKO.TXT	Describes program, conditions for use, and so on

A Screen-Blanker Sampler

      Fish, Magic, and Fireworks

In this chapter we introduce a number of graphically interesting display packages, all of which can be set up to blank your Windows display after a certain period of inactivity. Screen blankers are a very good idea and should be part of everyone's desktop because they're designed to exercise all areas of your computer's display equally and randomly.

By using a screen blanker, you can avoid leaving the same pattern on your display for long periods of time, thereby escaping the phenomenon known as phosphor burn-in. Over time, the ability of the screen to display information gets diminished by continued use; after years of displaying the same patterns, images actually etch their way into the display, showing up in ghostly fashion even when the screen is displaying other things. Using a screen blanker avoids this burn-in and prolongs the effective life of your equipment. Need we say more?

Of course we do! The *real* motivation behind screen blankers is to display all kinds of keen stuff on your display while the machine isn't busy doing other work. That's why we've picked three standouts from the dozens of interesting and entertaining screen blankers available for Windows.

A word of warning: It's best not to try to run more than one screen blanker at a time because of the ensuing confusion that can result. Try them individually and stick with the one that you like best (don't forget to send the registration fee). If you try them together, it could cause problems for some applications (for instance, we couldn't get our screen capture program, HiJaak, to work when multiple screen blankers were active).

 # Fish!

What Fish! Does

Fish! is our personal favorite out of the batch discussed here, primarily because it's the most fun. It turns your screen from a pane of pallid glass into a view of a fish tank filled with exotic fish. It is driven by a collection of animated fish definition files (of type .FSH, of course). Historical note: The original Mac version of Fish! appears in the first Stupid book, *Stupid Mac Tricks*.

Fish! even includes a nifty fish editor so you can design your own denizens of the deep or change the patterns of existing ones. The shareware version's fish editor has its Save feature disabled—although you can make all the fish you want, you can't keep them around (don't worry, we'll tell you how to obtain a registered copy below so you can save your fish).

The list of fish that Fish! can display is long and its inhabitants are colorful and interesting. They have to be seen in color to be truly appreciated, but they don't look too bad in monochrome either.

How to Use Fish!

Installing Fish! is made extremely easy by virtue of an install utility, named SETUP.EXE, that is included with the program and its fish definition files. Setup will copy the program and the .FSH files to your Windows directory, install the program in your WIN.INI file, and set up your first-time use.

When running Fish! you have the option of having fish swim on your desktop, in addition to setting a timeout after which the program's screen blanker goes into effect. Figure 6 shows the Preferences window for Fish!, which lets you select how many fish will be displayed at any one time, determines whether or not the desktop is aswim with fish, and lets you get to the Fish Menu depicted in Figure 7 with a click on the desktop. This last feature is very handy because it gives you an easy way to get to the Task List as well as to control your fish activities.

The screen-saver options for Fish! are shown in Figure 8. You may select a corner of the screen in which to throw yourself into the fish tank with Sleep Now mode, and another corner of the screen in which to disable the fish display with the Sleep Never mode. It's also possible to change the inactivity period from its default of 15 minutes to whatever works best for you. You can even set a password to control access to your computer once Fish! has taken over. This

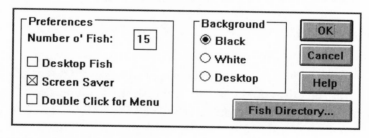

Figure 6: Fish! Preferences

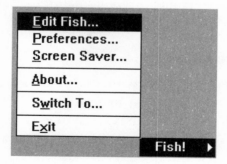

Figure 7: The Fish! Double-Click menu (selecting Double Click for Menu from Figure 6 causes this menu to be displayed whenever the desktop is double-clicked)

27

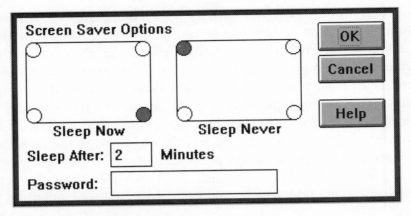

Figure 8: Fish! screen blanker controls

means that you can use Fish! to keep other people from using your computer—perhaps foiling a dirty trickster—by setting a password and making sure Fish! is active before leaving your machine.

Escaping Fish!

Getting out of Fish! is pretty easy: You can get to it through the Task List or by setting the double-click box in the Screen Saver window. This latter selection puts you into the Fish! menu when you double-click on the desktop. If you've used SETUP.EXE to make loading Fish! automatic and you want to change that, you'll have to remove the FISH statement from the Load= portion of your WIN.INI file. While you're at it, you should also eliminate the [FISH] section at the bottom of WIN.INI as well.

Fish!: The Fine Print

The version of Fish! supplied with this book is a shareware evaluation copy only. You may distribute it freely to friends and colleagues—you can even distribute it commercially, as long as you make it clear that the costs cover only the duplication and materials, not the program itself. Tom & Ed were also clever enough to write a great program in a shareware implementation that doesn't have the full functionality of the registered version (save those Fish!).

28

As with all the real shareware in this book, we strongly encourage you to register (save those Fish!). Registration costs $24.95 ($34.95 outside the U.S.), and should be in the form of a check or money order addressed to:

Tom & Ed's Bogus Software
Fish Shareware Upgrade
15600 NE 8th St., Suite A3334
Bellevue, WA 98008

Registration gets you a fully functional Fish! Editor and a larger menagerie of fish (and other beasts). If you use this program regularly, it's definitely worth the money.

Author's Comments

Fish! 3.0 by Ed Fries and Tom Saxton, is Copyright 1991, Tom & Ed's Bogus Software. At Bogus Software, we're not looking for credibility, we're looking for incredibility!

Fish!: The Files

*.FSH	Fish (and other creature) definition files: 26 in all
FISH.EXE	Screen blanker program
FISH.HLP	Help files for Fish! program
FISH!.INI	Text copied to WIN.INI file during Setup; defines creatures, file locations, and so on
FISHLIB.DLL	Library that supplies common animation routines, drawing/editing functions, and so on
README.TXT	ASCII text file describing program, conditions for use, and so on
SETUP.EXE	Windows installation program for Fish!
SETUP.INF	Text file that drives Setup's file transfers, edits, and so on

 **Magic**

What Magic Does

Magic works in much the same way as Fish!, but it offers an ever-changing pattern of colored lines that form moire patterns on the screen instead of a tank full of piscine creatures. In lieu of a fish editor, Magic offers a bit more in the way of screen controls and pattern mirroring, not to mention a flashier logo that can be animated, if desired.

How to Use Magic

The Magic install program is named INSTALL.EXE, and lives in the Magic directory: C:\WINDOWS\MAGIC. It can be invoked through the File Manager directly, or by using the Run command, as you like. The only advantage of using the install program is to make Magic a part of your regular Windows startup environment; for those who do not want to do this, Magic can also be invoked by starting the program, MAGIC.EXE, directly through the File Manager.

Figure 9 depicts the request that Magic makes. Please note that the install program also alters your WIN.INI file to automatically load Magic on startup. If you plan on trying out multiple screen blankers, you'll need to edit WIN.INI yourself to deinstall your previous screen blanker before installing a different one.

Figure 9: Magic's Install Window

30

Magic's repertoire of screen displays consists of animating a moving pattern of colored lines for moire effects or blanking the screen to dead blank (the authors recommend this latter approach in office environments where other workers might be distracted by patterns showing on a computer in a public area or shared work space).

Magic's Control Panel, depicted in Figure 10, might therefore appear to be a bit misleading when it offers multiple display effects for the Magic icon. These displays change only the appearance of the Magic icon when Magic is not active rather than changing the behavior of the program's screen-blanking effects. The three icons offered include a Magic icon, featuring a rabbit emerging from a hat; a Nova icon, which makes a bright flash just before Magic enters Sleep mode and takes over the screen; and a moire pattern, which displays a bright multicolored image when Magic is being manipulated but otherwise displays the moire pattern in animated miniature fashion.

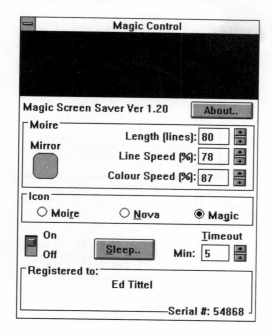

Figure 10: Magic's Control Panel

The real intent of the Control Panel is to control Magic's behavior: It permits the line length of the displays to be altered, and it manages the speed of motion on the screen and the speed of color shifts in the lines displayed. Again, we found the defaults to be satisfactory on all but the fastest machines, where we had to reduce the line-motion and color-shift speeds.

Clicking on the Sleep button in the Control Panel produces a window that lets you designate Sleep and Wake corners on your display (see Figure 11). Leaving the mouse inactive in the Sleep corner for more than one second automatically invokes Magic, while leaving the mouse in the Wake corner keeps Magic from activating no matter how long it stays there (which is useful for when you need to refer to what's on screen for an extended period of otherwise idle time).

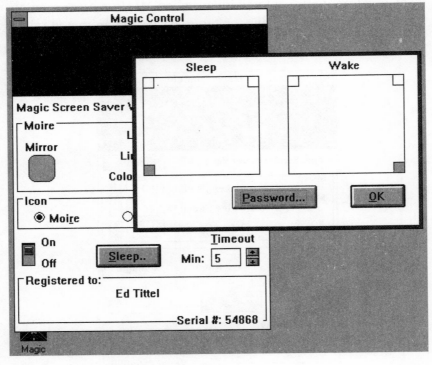

Figure 11: Magic's Sleep Window

The Sleep Window also gives access to a Password Window, where you can set a Magic password. Unlike Fish!, where turning off the machine permits the password to be bypassed on restart, Magic remembers if it was powered down with password protection required. In English this means that Magic's password protection is harder to beat than the scheme in Fish!. If others have access to your machine and security is a real concern, Magic's password abilities can be a real boon.

We're hard-pressed to recommend Fish! over Magic or vice-versa: Fish! clearly wins in the diverting displays category, but Magic is more effective as a workaday screen blanker. Try them out for yourself to decide which you prefer.

Escaping Magic

As a well-behaved Windows application, you can exit Magic through any of the normal methods: Control-Escape to get to the Task List, selecting Exit through the Control button, or Alt-F4 while the program is active to force it to quit.

Magic: The Fine Print

The author's comments for Magic tell most of what you need to know about the product. To contact Software Dynamics regarding Magic or their development services, you can write, call, or FAX:

Software Dynamics
5221 Central Avenue
Bayside Park, Suite 8
Richmond, CA 94804
Voice: (510) 524-9027; FAX: (510) 528-1456

The only information that's missing from their comments is that registering Magic costs $20. It entitles you to registration in the Software Dynamics database and includes instructions on how to personalize your copy and a registration number. If you want Software Dynamics to send a copy of the program on disk, please add an additional $5 to your check or money order.

Author's Comments

The Magic Screen Saver for Windows was developed by Bill Stewart and Ian MacDonald of Software Dynamics, a Windows software development company based in Calgary, Alberta. Magic was so popular that Software Dynamics later developed the ultimate screen saver for Windows, After Dark [Editor's note: After Dark is also available for the Macintosh]. *After Dark Windows is a commercial application published through Berkeley Systems. Magic is still supported and is available on online services or direct from Software Dynamics.*

The authors would like to thank the thousands of Magic users worldwide for supporting our development and the shareware concept.

Magic: The Files

INSTALL.EXE	Program that installs Magic
MAGIC.EXE	Magic screen-saver program
MAGIC.WRI	Magic documentation (worth reading!)
MAGICLIB.DLL	Magic Dynamic Link Library; provides draw and animation capabilities
TECHSTUF.WRI	Additional technical information on Magic

 **Fireworks**

What Fireworks Does

Fireworks is the last of our triumvirate of screen blankers. It distinguishes itself from the other two by being freeware. While this program doesn't have as many bells and whistles as its companions in this chapter, no one can say the price isn't right! Fireworks also earns a place in our hearts because its inspiration was a Macintosh program called Pyro! that we both used as our very first screen blanker back in the mid-eighties. This bit of nostalgia might not be worth much to you, but it did get our attention!

One interesting aspect of Fireworks' behavior is the way it treats the cursor when it enters its window: It turns the pointer shape into an airplane. If you also happen to click on a mouse button while the cursor is in this form, it drops a bomb that explodes when it hits the window's lower edge and causes the screen display to flash in response to the explosion. This is a harmless, but entertaining, elaboration of the fireworks metaphor.

How to Use Fireworks

Installing Fireworks is very easy: Simply double-click on the FIREWORK.EXE file in the File Manager or use the Run command to fire it off. Fireworks starts up in a modestly sized window with Setup as the only menu choice, as shown in Figure 12. This menu lets you set Fireworks' mode of operation, establish the idle delay period before its screen blanking cuts in, and determine any of a number of hotkeys to control the program's behavior.

Fireworks can also be run in full-screen mode by pressing the Ctrl and F keys simultaneously; this causes Fireworks to take over the entire display (great for using as a screen blanker for extended periods). To recover the screen, you must then either click in the upper left-hand corner of the screen or press the Alt and spacebar keys simultaneously.

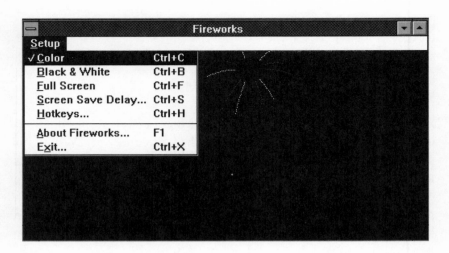

Figure 12: Starting up Fireworks

Hotkeys can be used to control Fireworks pretty much completely, including selections to force the screen to blank immediately (the default is Alt-Control); to enable auto-blanking (the default is Alt-Keypad Plus and is used to tell Fireworks to act as a screen blanker); and to disable auto-blanking (the default is Alt-Keypad Minus and is used to tell Fireworks not to blank the screen). In other words, these controls are analogous to the function of the Sleep and Wake corners that both Magic and Fish! use to control their activity. As Figure 13 illustrates, Fireworks offers an ample variety of hotkey settings for each command should the defaults conflict with hotkeys set up for other Windows programs.

To make Fireworks a regular part of your Windows environment, edit the Run= section of your WIN.INI file to include a path reference to FIREWORK.EXE, for example,

Run=C:\WINDOWS\FIREWORK\FIREWORK.EXE

would reference the program as installed using the defaults supplied by our batch-file installer. To have Windows blank your screen automatically on startup, add a /B parameter to the line above.

36

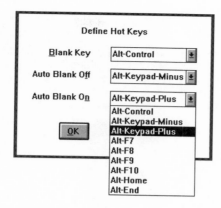

Figure 13: Fireworks' hotkey selections

Escaping Fireworks

Getting out of Fireworks is just as easy as double-clicking on the icon (or the top-left command button, if you've got the Fireworks window open) and selecting Close (Alt-F4 also works, in typical Windows fashion).

Fireworks: The Fine Print

Fireworks is the work of Kim Levitt of Synergistic Enterprises. The author can be contacted at:

Synergistic Enterprises
8033 Sunset Blvd. #975
Los Angeles, CA 90046

The author's comments are a quote from the documentation file for the program that explains conditions for its use.

Author's Comments

Fireworks v5.40 is being released as a "freeware" program, which means you do not have to pay the author or register the program. You are free to use and copy this program to share with friends, but no money other than a minimal amount to cover duplicating costs should be charged and I ask that this document file be included unaltered, along with the FIRELIB.DLL dynamic link library file.

37

If you have a modem, by all means check out the Synergistic Enterprises BBS system at (213) 653-6398. Set your modem to 8 bits, no parity, 1 stop bit. The system is up 24 hours a day, 7 days a week (except during maintenance). Enjoy!

Fireworks: The Files

FIRE54.WRI	Documentation file for Fireworks v5.4
FIRELIB.DLL	Dynamic link library for Fireworks display and animation
FIREWORK.EXE	Fireworks program
README.TXT	ASCII text file describing Fireworks files

ANNOY

 Nasties Attack the Desktop

What ANNOY Does

In the purest form of self-advertisement imaginable, ANNOY lives up to its name. It includes two programs that violate Windows etiquette and write patterns at random anywhere on the screen instead of opening their own windows and sticking within their confines. The first program, BURST.EXE, writes a starburst pattern that's intended to look like little dings on the desktop; the second program, FACE.EXE, does the same thing, except that it scrawls obnoxious little faces all over the place instead.

How to Use ANNOY

With either program, use the File Manager to get to the directory where BURST.EXE or FACE.EXE lives (C:\WINDOWS\ANNOY), and then double-click on that file or use the Run command to set either or both of them off. The screen goes crazy when both are running at the same time, so it's worth trying just for grins.

A word of warning: Both BURST.EXE and FACE.EXE were compiled under an earlier version of Windows. This means that when you fire them up, you'll get a warning screen that asks you if you really want to run this outmoded software or not, as depicted in Figure 14. While the warnings are dire, the behavior of the programs in our testing seemed fairly benign: Even with a couple of heavy-duty applications running in Enhanced mode, adding either BURST or FACE to the mix did not cause any ill effects.

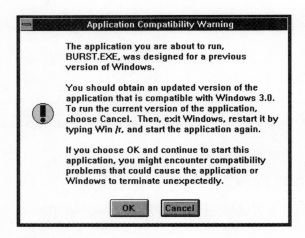

Figure 14: Warning screen

Escaping ANNOY

Unfortunately, there is no way out until ANNOY has its way with you. Each program keeps writing its little symbols to the screen until 100 have been scrawled in one place or another. At this point a window opens that asks the question "Had enough?," as shown in Figure 15. Selecting Yes causes either program to terminate and remove itself from the Windows environment. For all but real masochists, one helping of 100 faces or burst marks is more than enough. Please note the background to the "Had enough?" window: It shows what BURST's handiwork looks like.

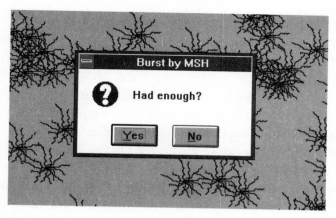

Figure 15: Had enough?

Suggestions for Using ANNOY

ANNOY begs to be put on some unsuspecting person's desktop, to wreak its havoc in a mysterious manner. However, the warning screen depicted in Figure 14 is a dead giveaway that something fishy might be up. The only underhanded method for springing this on someone else is to have a confederate who can distract the hapless target while you fire up FACE or BURST and get past that screen; otherwise, ANNOY is just an interesting demonstration that graphics don't necessary have to stay within the frame of a particular window even if they haven't taken over the screen completely.

In order to pull off the dastardly deed we propose, you'll have to copy the files BURST.EXE and FACE.EXE onto your target's machine before arranging a distraction; otherwise, your confederate will have to come up with a distraction that takes long enough to handle the file copy as well as the invocation. Of course, if you can find somebody who runs Windows in Real mode anyway, this trick is made for that environment and can be used without any of the shenanigans we've suggested.

ANNOY: The Fine Print

ANNOY is freeware, originally developed by Michael Harrison, and cleaned up further by Perri Nelson. ANNOY can be copied and distributed freely, but we encourage would-be tricksters to trick responsibly. The least you can do for your victim—errr, target—is to stick around and let them know that you've seen this kind of thing before and it goes away by itself after a while.

The original author can be contacted via CompuServe as follows:
Michael Harrison: 76057,101

At the time we went to press, we were not able to locate Perri Nelson, but we hope this book will cause him (or her) to make himself (or herself) known!

ANNOY: The Files

BURST.EXE	Burst program file
FACE.EXE	Face program file
README.WRI	Perri Nelson's commentary on the programs
README.TXT	Michael Harrison's short description of the programs

Icon Frightener

 Catch It If You Can

What Icon Frightener Does

Scott Gourley, the author of Icon Frightener, is a man after our own hearts: He announces the program as a gimmick that may ultimately find its place one day in the "Windows Un-Productivity Pack." In his terminology, Icon Frightener provides a method of afflicting the icons on the Windows desktop with "cursorphobia" so that whenever you try to click the cursor on an icon, the icon jumps away. Sort of like Sisyphus, but no hills or boulder in sight.

How to Use Icon Frightener

Installing Icon Frightener is the essence of simplicity: Just double-click on the program ICOFRITE.EXE in the File Manager or use it as the argument to the Run command box. That's all there is to it. You'll then proceed to amuse yourself by chasing your icons around the desktop. (Note: Icon Frightener only works on icons for active programs—that is, icons on the desktop—not on icons of programs in the Program Manager or the groups of programs that it manages.)

The best way to get the full effect of Icon Frightener is to have plenty of desktop to chase things around in while you become familiar with the program. The most straightforward way to do this is to minimize all the pieces of your desktop, as depicted in Figure 16 (before chasing). When you chase the icons around, they become separated from their title blocks, as depicted in Figure 17 (after chasing).

Figure 16: Before the Icons get frightened

Figure 17: After the Icons get frightened

The important thing about using Icon Frightener is not to panic: It's not really doing anything to your desktop except moving graphics around.

Hint: You can still open any icon by double-clicking on its title bar; although the icon moves to elude your cursor, the title bar stays put! Notice, though, that when the desktop gets repainted after you halt the Icon Frightener program, the title bars move to where the icons are, not the other way around.

Escaping Icon Frightener

There are several methods for escaping from Icon Frightener, and they all depend on the same end result: using the Task List to end the Icon Frightener task. This may be accomplished by double-clicking on any icon title bar and using the Switch-to selection in the control menu, by double-clicking the desktop to call up the Task List directly, or by entering Ctrl-Esc at the keyboard to access the Task List through its hotkey invocation.

Suggestions for Using Icon Frightener

While there's really not much to Icon Frightener, it does provide quite a bit of amusement, even if you use it only on yourself. And as a very safe trick with no negative side effects, it's prime material for inflicting on others.

Hint: If you install Icon Frightener on someone else's machine, hide the Icon Frightener icon afterwards by chasing it to the edge of the screen or underneath an open window. It's amazing how long people will chase after their icons before realizing that something's amiss and making use of the escape methods we just described.

As always, if you're going to play tricks on other people, we strongly recommend that you do so responsibly. Stick around and be ready to help the person with frightened icons recover from their strange and interesting malady.

Icon Frightener: The Fine Print

Icon Frightener is freeware and can be copied and distributed as you like.

ICOFRITE Version 2.0 Icon Frightener for Microsoft Windows
Copyright © 1991 Scott Gourley/ Clickon Software
105 Union Street
Watertown, MA 02172
CompuServe ID 72311,613

Icon Frightener is the brainchild of Scott Gourley of Clickon Software, whose own comments from the documentation file, ICOFRITE.DOC, sum up his attitude toward providing such great software diversions.

Author's Comments

This program is freeware, but if you would like any more of this type of program from me, please feel free to send any size donation! I have several more ideas for Windows gimmicks—perhaps I'll put together a collection and call it the "Windows Un-productivity Pack."

Icon Frightener: The Files

FRITE.DLL	Dynamic link library for screen updates
ICOFRITE.DOC	Documentation for program
ICOFRITE.EXE	Icon Frightener program

Gatling

 A Windows Shoot-'em-Up!

What Gatling Does

Gatling blows metaphorical holes in your screen while emitting a machine-gun-like sound. To our way of thinking, it is the ultimate Stupid Windows Trick in this collection: a simple-minded violation of the sanctity (and quiet) of the workaday desktop.

The full name of the product is the Gatling Machine Gun Screen Blaster. It's a real mouthful, but it really says it all. Gatling is timed to go off periodically, shooting a hail of bullets at your screen and leaving behind a trail of bullet holes.

How to Use Gatling

Using Gatling requires that you exercise the now-familiar litany of program launching in Windows: through the File Manager, double-click the file named GATLING.EXE. Then stick around until the shooting starts. Of course, you could use the File Manager's Run command:

Run C:\WINDOWS\GATLING\GATLING.EXE

47

If you'd like to keep your desktop full of holes, you could even put the same reference in your WIN.INI file, in the Run= section, to load the program when Windows starts up.

Escaping Gatling

If you can find the Gatling icon, a single click brings up its control menu as depicted in Figure 18; you can then click on Close or strike Alt-F4 to end the program. If you can't find the icon, double-click on the desktop or hit Alt-Esc to call up the Task List, highlight Gatling, and then click on End Task. What could be easier? The nice thing about Gatling is that it's totally benign, even if it does ventilate your display from time to time.

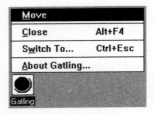

Figure 18: Gatling controls

Suggestions for Using Gatling

After you've shot yourself a few times—and who doesn't, just for practice—you'll want to share this program with your friends. The best way to do that is to secretly install and launch the program on somebody else's machine and then to slide the Gatling icon behind an open window so it's not immediately obvious what's going on (that's why we had to tell you how to deal with Gatling when the icon isn't visible).

Scott Gourley, the program's author, also recommends installing Gatling for those all-nighter marathon sessions at the keyboard when any assistance in staying awake is greatly appreciated. We tried it a couple of times and can endorse its caffeinelike effects! If you look at Figure 19, you'll see why it might startle a viewer into a less comatose state, especially when accompanied by shoot-'em-up sound effects.

48

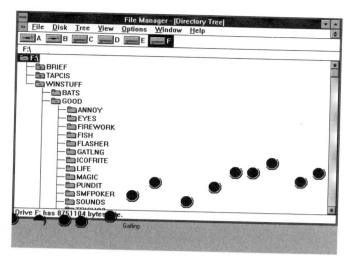

Figure 19: What Gatling leaves behind is holes

Gatling: The Fine Print

Although Gatling is shareware, there is no particular charge associated with it: Scott Gourley simply requests that you send him whatever you think is fair for the trick (we recommend $5). Feel free to share copies of the trick with your friends; just make sure the documentation file goes along with the program.

Gatling Version 2.0 Machine Gun Screen Blaster for Microsoft Windows.

Copyright © 1991 Scott Gourley/ Clickon Software
CompuServe ID 72311,613
105 Union Street
Watertown, MA 02172

Gatling: The Files

GATLING.DOC	ASCII text file describing the program
GATLING.EXE	Gatling Machine Gun Screen Blaster program

Pundit

 Sayings from Chairman Bill?

What Pundit Does

Pundit is a form of "fortune cookie" program that runs quietly on your desktop and regularly flashes an inspirational message at you in a small, well-behaved window. It's a simple-minded but diverting form of Windows entertainment drawn from a wide range of sources—from Groucho Marx to Winston Churchill—that will be sure to keep you amused.

How to Use Pundit

Firing off Pundit follows the standard Windows application-launch scenario: Double-click on the PUNDIT.EXE file or use the Run command to set the program in motion. This will bring up the first of many quote windows that Pundit will flash to your screen. Since these windows don't stick around very long—the default is 5 seconds—you'll want to click on the Choices entry in the Menu title bar right away because this is how you get at Pundit's controls (under the Choices menu heading), as shown in Figure 20.

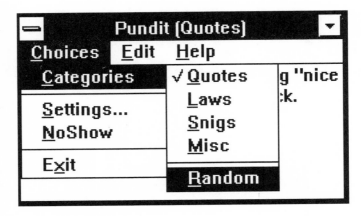

Figure 20: Pundit controls

In Figure 20, we've highlighted the hierarchical menu for the categories that the quotes are broken into. You can elect to view quotes from any of four categories. These categories are:

- Quotes. This is the program default and includes about 100 quotes selected by the program's author for display.

- Laws. Murphy's Law (with many humorous special cases) and other related laws of nature and humanity.

- Snigs. Definitions of unreal words, à la *Not Necessarily the News'* Rich Hall.

- Misc. Miscellaneous sayings that didn't fit any of the categories above but were included anyway.

While each of the categories for sayings or quotes is pretty interesting, we liked the Random selection at the bottom of the Categories list the best because it chooses from all four categories and grants a bit more range to Pundit's behavior.

What Pundit offers by way of settings is short and sweet: There's a setting for how long quotes stay on the screen that can vary from 1 to 60 seconds (Seconds In) and a setting for how long between quotes that can vary from 20 to 3,600 seconds (Seconds Out). Our experiments showed us that the default for display time works fine: It gives enough time to read the longest quote without hanging around long enough to be a nuisance. The 20-second interval between quotes was too short for our taste; we found it worked better when set to approximately 5 minutes (300 seconds, or thereabout). In addition, there is a set of color controls to set the foreground (text and window components) and background (inside of window) colors. Figure 21 depicts a sample quote and the Settings window. Please notice how the Random mode gets included in the program's title bar to let you know what mode you're in.

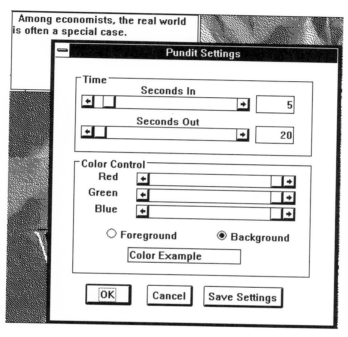

Figure 21: Pundit settings and sample quote

Once you've made your selections, there are three buttons to choose from to exit the Pundit Settings window: OK accepts the settings but makes them effective only for your current session; Cancel ignores whatever changes you've made and closes the controls; and Save Settings writes the new values to your WIN.INI file in a section named [jkbPundit] for use whenever you run Pundit in the future. If you do elect to Save Settings, you will have to click on the OK or Cancel button to exit the control window once the settings have been recorded in your WIN.INI file.

53

The final item on the choices menu is a NoShow submenu. This lets you decide whether or not you want Pundit to show on your desktop as an icon while it's between sayings. The two choices under NoShow are Iconize and Hide. Choosing Iconize is what makes Pundit appear as an icon between sayings; choosing Hide causes Pundit to be invisible when it's not actively displaying a message on your screen. We much preferred using Iconize because it lets us get at Pundit even when it's not onscreen to turn it off or to change its behavior. In Hide mode the only time you can get at Pundit's controls is when it's displaying something on the screen. Figure 22 depicts the NoShow menu.

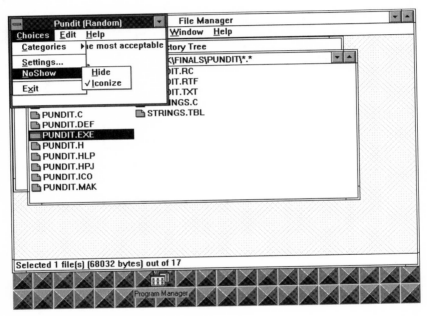

Figure 22: Pundit's NoShow menu

The main Pundit menu also supports two other choices: Edit, which lets you copy the quote or saying on display to the clipboard, and Help, which explains the program's behavior from within Microsoft's standard Help environment.

There's also a good documentation file for Pundit included with the program called PUNDIT.TXT. We'd recommend that you either browse the Help information or read this file to become more fully acquainted with Pundit when you first install it. Even though the program is fairly simpleminded, it does offer some interesting options and capabilities. Since Pundit includes the source code, programmers will find PUNDIT.TXT especially interesting because it talks about the design motivation and some creative ways the program might be customized.

Escaping Pundit

In Hide mode Pundit does not register itself as a task running under the Task List, except when it's actually showing onscreen. When the program is in this mode, the only way to turn Pundit off is to grab a Quote window while it's onscreen, get into the menu, and select the Exit option. If you can grab the Task List while a Quote window is showing, you can then use the End Task button to halt the program, but if the window is showing you can use its menu just as well.

This, of course, is why we recommend using the Iconize approach to run Pundit—it doesn't require that you grab a window whenever it does show up. It also means that you don't have to be concerned about the Seconds In setting that controls how long a saying will actually stay on screen.

If you do elect to put Pundit on somebody else's desktop in Hide mode, it's not really sporting if the display time is set to less than 3 seconds or so: We mere mortals aren't fast enough to get the mouse positioned and clicked in such a short time. If this should happen by accident—as it did during our testing—the only way to solve the problem if the settings have been saved is to edit WIN.INI with Notepad and to change the value assigned to the variable named InSecs to a higher number, save the file, and then exit and restart Windows. If the settings are temporary, you'll only need to exit Windows and restart because the previous settings (or defaults) will take over when you restart the program in the next Windows session.

Suggestions for Using Pundit

Pundit has as rightful a place on your own desktop as on somebody else's because of its entertainment value. Because it doesn't show up as a task under the Task List in Hide mode, it is a particularly good trick to play on Windows Wizards. They'll try to catch and kill it using the normal Windows task management techniques for a while before figuring out that grabbing the quote window is the only way to halt the program.

If you're intrepid enough to make the effort—and have access to a Microsoft C compiler and the Windows Software Developer's Kit (SDK)—you can even rebuild the program with your own customized messages. This gives you unlimited freedom to tailor the quotes to your own desktop, or somebody else's, for a truly refined form of trickery. As always, remember to trick responsibly and to be there to help out if needed.

Finally, if you are a Windows programmer, you will find the source code for Pundit that is included along with the files in C:\WINDOWS\PUNDIT of considerable interest because Pundit was written to exercise Windows' little-used facility to create private message streams, especially for displaying the Quote windows.

Pundit: The Fine Print

Jeff Bienstadt, the author of Pundit, provides the essential details in his documentation file, PUNDIT.TXT, so we recommend reading that at least once.

Because Pundit is copyrighted shareware that has been made available for distribution by the author, you may share copies of it with others, but please read PUNDIT.TXT for the restrictions that apply to its distribution.

Jeff Bienstadt
13305 NE 171st Street, #D130
Woodinville, WA 98072

Author's Comments

Pundit is a ShareWare program. If you find this program (or the accompanying source code) useful, please send a check for $5.

From PUNDIT.TXT, we add the following:

If you have any questions or comments about this program, I would love to hear from you (this includes Windows Wizards with comments about how to improve it). I can be reached at the above address or on CompuServe at 72200,3477.

Pundit: The Files

EXTRAS.C	C source for some Windows extras
EXTRAS.H	Include files for Windows extras
PUNDIT	Pundit Make file (for NMAKE)
PUNDIT.C	C source code for Pundit program
PUNDIT.DEF	Linker definitions to build Pundit program
PUNDIT.EXE	Pundit program file
PUNDIT.H	C include file that defines program constants
PUNDIT.HLP	Pundit Help file
PUNDIT.HPJ	The Help Project File (for HC)
PUNDIT.ICO	Icon file
PUNDIT.RC	Pundit resource file (includes quotations)
PUNDIT.RTF	Source for the help file
PUNDIT.TXT	Pundit documentation file (worth reading!)
SETTINGS.C	C source code for the settings dialog, and so on
STRINGS.TBL	String table (with quotations)

LIFE

 A Mathematical Diversion or Animated Art?

What LIFE Does

LIFE is a mathematical recreation that first made its appearance on the pages of *Scientific American* back in the late sixties. Its earliest implementations were painfully slow because they had to be worked out by hand on graph paper. As implemented here, the computer does all the work and animates the process for you so that you can simply watch the patterns move across the screen. We're not sure if this trick is really stupid or not because of its mathematical basis and scientific interest, but it makes one heck of an interesting-looking screen display. (As some wag put it: "That's LIFE!")

How to Use LIFE

Under Windows, LIFE gets started in the File Manager with a double-click on the file named C:\WINDOWS\LIFE\LIFE.EXE, or through its use as the argument to the Run command.

The title bar on the game's window reads LIFE, and we shall now proceed to explain how LIFE is played, first mathematically, and then in terms of this implementation.

In mathematical terms, the playing field consists of a matrix of squares, some of which are filled in as "live cells," the remainder of which are "dead cells." By default, dead cells are white and live cells colored, where a progression of colors indicates the "age" of a given cell.

Each turn of the game is called a generation and consists of analyzing the relative positions of live and dead cells to determine which cells are live and which ones are dead in that generation. The rules are simple, but we'll cover them broadly by saying that only cells with exactly three adjacent neighbors live on, while those with more or fewer die. In fact, some configurations appear to cause cells to "move" across generations rather than to stay put, but these general observations hold pretty well for the game.

As you watch the game over time, you'll observe two categories of interesting configurations: stable ones that don't move or change as long as they're not "touched" by moving configurations, and moving configurations that maintain a constant pattern but move around the playing field. Those readers who are interested in all of the gory details should consult John Horton Conway's book *On Numbers and Games* (Academic Press, London, 1976). Conway is the man who invented the game of LIFE and his description is the ultimate definition. We're more interested in how to make the program run, so we'll proceed to cover that now.

Figure 23 depicts the LIFE Window, where the controls occupy the menu bar. Reading from left to right, we see:

- Run, which lets you animate the playing field or step through generations one at a time.

- Options, which sets the conditions of the playing field as follows:

Clear (CTRL C)	clears all occupied cells
Gridlines off (CTRL G)	turns off matrix lines
Timer (CTRL T)	sets the life cycle per generation
Small Grid (CTRL S)	shows small cells onscreen

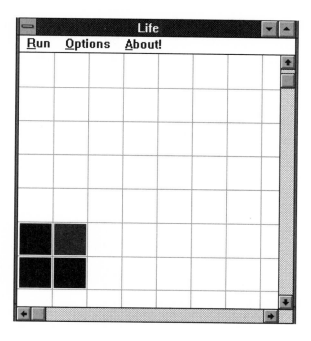

Figure 23: Life at Work

Medium Grid (CTRL M)   shows medium-sized cells on-screen

Large Grid (CTRL G)   shows large-sized cells onscreen

- About, which shows a short information window about LIFE.

Escaping LIFE

The usual techniques for escaping the program work very nicely: Use Close or Alt-F4 from the Control button to have the program stop itself, or use Alt-Esc or double-click on the desktop to get into the Task List to have it halt the program. Either way, it's pretty well behaved.

61

Suggestions for Using LIFE

Those readers interested in the game of LIFE itself will find this computerized version a useful tool for examining the game and becoming more familiar with it. For such aficionados we especially recommend Conway's book: It depicts a number of recognized stable and moving configurations that you can key in using the hand-shaped cursor and play with to your heart's content.

One big difference between LIFE as defined mathematically by Conway and LIFE as implemented in this program is that the program is set up to age cells across generations, and it kills off any cells after they live through a number of generations. In the game as defined by Conway, no aging process exists: Cells either live or die only based on the number of adjacent neighbors. The following color progression will help you to observe the aging scheme in LIFE as implemented here (LIFE uses different gray-scales for each color mentioned below on gray-scale monochrome displays, but there is no equivalent for pure monochrome displays):

Medium green	Initial generation
Light blue	Phase 2
Maroon	Phase 3
Purple	Phase 4
Light green	Phase 5
Dark blue	Phase 6

After the cells turn dark blue, they disappear (unless refreshed by a nearby neighbor).

LIFE can consume a large amount of computing resources, so if you do decide to use it as a pseudo-screenblanker or as a distractor in an unoccupied region of the screen, we suggest that you set the timer to a relatively long interval (500 milliseconds or greater) and that you select large cell sizes for the display. The longer interval and the larger cells will consume less CPU power, leaving more left over for other things to happen. We noticed that with the screen completely filled with LIFE and small cells, even our fastest machine—a 486/33 MHz—slowed down appreciably.

For hedonists interested purely in the entertainment side of LIFE, fire it up, pick Run, click Start, and sit back and watch those patterns crawl! Tightly shrunk, it makes an interesting distractor tucked into a corner of your display. If you have a color monitor, watching the color combinations of aging cells and stretching it to fill most of your screen will turn it into a nice pseudo-screen-blanker.

LIFE: The Fine Print

LIFE is freeware entered into the public domain by its author, Thomas Wheeler. Please notice that the files include C language source code, for those who wish to examine the program more closely. This program may be freely shared with others, so long as it includes all of the files stipulated in the README.TXT file for its distribution.

Those wishing to reach Thomas Wheeler with comments or suggestions about LIFE can do so via CompuServe at 72037,1742, or at the following address:

Thomas D. Wheeler
31294 Morlock
Livonia, MI 48152

LIFE: The Files

HAND.CUR	Definition file for the hand-shaped cursor used to edit cell configurations
LIFE.C	C-language source code for LIFE program
LIFE.DEF	Code and data definitions for LIFE program
LIFE.EXE	LIFE program
LIFE.H	Include file for LIFE program
LIFE.ICO	Definition for LIFE icon
LIFE.MAK	Make file for building LIFE executable

LIFE.OBJ	LIFE object file (for linking LIFE executable)
LIFE.RC	Resource file for LIFE program
LIFE.RES	LINK file of LIFE program resources
LIFE.STS	Borland Programmer's Workbench LIFE environment
README.TXT	LIFE documentation file (worth reading)

SMF Casino Poker

 **Good Thing It's "Funny Money," Honey!**

What SMF Casino Poker Does

SMF Casino Poker is a true-to-life implementation of the video poker machines found in Atlantic City. It offers a wide variety of betting and playing options and is seriously addicting. Be warned: If you're not careful, that could be you staring at the screen at 2 in the morning wondering where the time has gone. We know!

How to Use SMF Casino Poker

Double-click the icon for SMFPOKER.EXE, or use the Run command to fire off the game, and you're ready to play. Once you've launched the application, you'll find yourself looking at a window papered in official "gambling green"—don't ask us why, but this is the color you'll find as the background for most PC gambling games.

The menu titles announce your options; beneath it is a status block that indicates your remaining funds, the value of each coin, the number of coins to be bet, and (for the truly dim-witted) the value of each bet. Alongside the status block you'll find a list of payouts for winning hands. At the bottom of the window is a five-card hand, face-down, ready to be dealt. All of this is depicted in Figure 24.

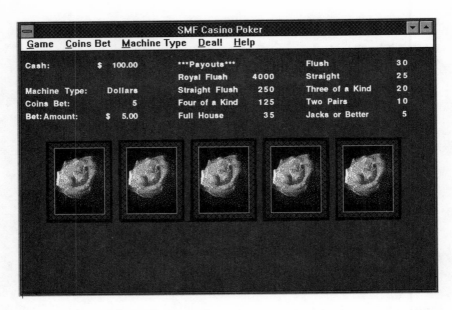

Figure 24: SMF Casino Poker controls

Before getting lost in play, let us fill you in on what the game controls offer, reading the menu bar from left to right:

- Game is used to control play and environment. Your choices are: New Game, which lets you start over when you're tapped out; Text Color, which sets text and card border colors; Background Color, which sets the color of the playing table; and Exit, which ends the game and returns you to the previous program.
- Coins Bet is the number of coins bet, from one to five.
- Machine Type denotes coins—quarters, halves, or dollars.
- Deal! deals a fresh hand.
- Help indicates available index- or browser-driven help (worth reading, too!).

Simply reading about the controls doesn't do justice to the feel and flow of the game, but it should cover the basics.

While you'll quickly establish a rhythm of your own when playing the game, we found it works best to use the keyboard rather than the mouse to handle play—there's a lot less motion involved, and that makes for much faster hands.

Once the game has started, striking the Alt and D keys simultaneously deals a fresh hand, while Return works best for the draw re-deal; in between, the numbered keys on the main keyboard let you select which cards to hold against your draw. While we wish that the keypad also worked to select cards to hold (it doesn't), keyboard-based play still flowed more smoothly for us than mouse-based play. Figure 25 shows what a hand in play looks like—after we elected to hold the pair of Kings we were initially dealt.

Figure 25: A hand in play

Escaping SMF Casino Poker

As a well-behaved Windows application, SMF Casino Poker supports all the well-known ways to quit: You can use the control button and close the game, you can select Exit from the Game menu bar, or you can get into the Task List and end the SMF Casino Poker task. It's getting out with your hide—and your bankroll—intact that's the tricky part! See Figure 26 for a reasonably common occurrence for us when we whiled away the hours "testing" this game.

Figure 26: Busted again!

Suggestions for Using SMF Casino Poker

Because the payouts and odds for playing poker are well documented in the game's Help files and in a whole slew of gambling books, we can't presume to tell you how best to play or how to get rich with the game, either.

The latest version of the game, delivered to us in September, 1991, included a new feature called Double Up that proved to be our undoing. If you win a hand, you have the option of doubling up: If you elect to double up, the dealer deals a five-card hand and turns the leftmost card up; you must turn one other card over. If that card is greater than or equal to the dealer's card, you've just doubled your winnings; if not, you've lost them and your original bet. We got cleaned out through this option a lot more than we should have, so we'd advise you to exercise caution. It can lead to that well-known phenomenon: "Even when I win, I lose!"

Seriously, though, the program's Help file is chock full of good advice on strategies for maximizing your winnings. It's worth reading through as you get to know the game and should help your overall rate of return.

SMF Casino Poker: The Fine Print

If you have any questions or comments, you can always reach the author via CompuServe E-mail at 76040,33 or via U.S. Mail at:

Paul D'Ascensio
SMF Softworks
33F Hillcroft/Clapboard Ridge
Danbury, CT 06811

68

The author's comments provide most of the useful information about SMF Casino Poker. The only thing we can add is that an order form is included with the files for the game, and that the cost of registration is $10.

Author's Comments

SMF Casino Poker is an evolving shareware program. By evolving, I mean that it is constantly being improved. By shareware, I mean it is available in a complete, not crippled, state to everyone who would like to try it out. All that I ask is if you like it and plan to use it, that you register it. The minimal registration fee goes toward future development and support. As a bonus, all registered users will receive the next version free and also have the opportunity to beta test future versions and other future projects.

I wish to thank everybody who has registered and offered suggestions to improve SMF Casino Poker. Without you, the game would be nothing.

PaulD

SMF Casino Poker: The Files

HISTORY.TXT	Revision history for the game
README.TXT	Brief overview of game and files
REGISTER.DOC	Order form to register
SMFPOKER.EXE	SMF Casino Poker program
SMFPOKER.HLP	SMF Casino Poker online Help files

Triangle Chaos

It's a Fractal Gas(ket)

What Triangle Chaos Does

Triangle Chaos dithers its way through a fractal program to show how order can be formed out of chaos. The name of the figure that gets drawn is a Serpinski Gasket, named after one of the mathematicians who worked on the mathematical study of chaos we now know as fractal geometry (well before Benoit Mandelbrot gave that branch of mathematics its name). Lest the whole theme seem too abstruse for our book, we hasten to add that we include this program because it draws neat pictures!

How to Use Triangle Chaos

We can use any of the standard Windows application-launching techniques to start the program, named TRICHO3.EXE. If we use the file manager to enter the directory C:\WINDOWS\TRICHO3, we need only double-click on the filename or enter the program's name as the argument to the Run Command.

The lone menu item inside Triangle Color deals with color selections for how the gasket gets displayed: It gives a choice of Black on White (the default); White on Black; Red, White, and Blue (for you real patriots); and Random Colors. Figure 27 shows a rendition of the figure filling up about one-quarter of a VGA screen. We found that a full-screen display of the program in random colors makes a pretty good pseudo screen blanker because the individual pixels in the image change color pretty regularly as the algorithm continues drawing the gasket, spiraling ever inward to infinity.

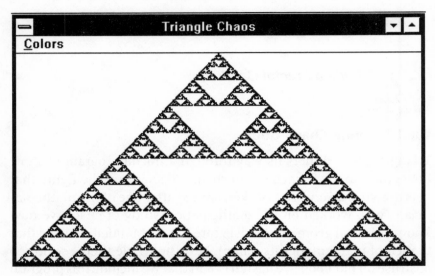

Figure 27: Triangle Chaos depicted

Minimizing the program to its icon also provides a neat animated display on your desktop, but because we can't reproduce color images in the book, we'll forgo showing it to you. If you have a color monitor then try it—you'll like it!

Warning: If you have a CGA monitor, the program may act strangely. It was designed only for EGA and VGA, so we don't recommend that you use it on a CGA.

Escaping Triangle Chaos

The control button offers a Close option to exit the program, or you can use the Alt-F4 keyboard equivalent. Likewise, using any of the techniques we've already described for getting to the Task List and then ending the Triangle Chaos task will also halt the program.

Suggestions for Using Triangle Chaos

Use it. Watch it. Enjoy it. We'd rank this trick with the other mathematically derived gem in this book—LIFE—in that it can be enjoyed for how it looks as much or more than for what it does. Don't take it too seriously, though. It's just another example of what crunching numbers can lead to!

If you're a programmer, you might want to take a look through the C source code for the program, which the author has provided for your perusal. It's interesting how such a simple algorithm can produce such a complex image.

Triangle Chaos: The Fine Print

Triangle Chaos is the brainchild of Marty Belles, who gets his jollies programming in his spare time. The program is freeware, so you may distribute it however you might like, provided that all the files are kept together and intact.

Marty can be contacted via CompuServe at 72735,661. He was kind enough to build us a fresh version for the book, and we'd like to take this opportunity to add our thanks for his hard work.

Author's Comments

Name:	*Marty Belles*
Hometown:	*Savannah, GA*
Occupation:	*Manufacturing Engineer for Gulfstream Aerospace*
Miscellaneous:	*I program as a hobby for both Windows and DOS. I use C as my primary language, with some assembly language.*

Triangle Chaos: The Files

TRICHO3	Make files to build the executable file
TRICHO3.C	C source code for program
TRICHO3.DEF	Linker definitions to build object files
TRICHO3.DOC	Program documentation
TRICHO3.EXE	Triangle Chaos program
TRICHO3.H	C include files to define common data structures
TRICHO3.ICO	Triangle Chaos icon definition
TRICHO3.RC	Common resource definitions for program

Wallpaper Randomizer

 Time to Redecorate

What Wallpaper Randomizer Does

Wallpaper Randomizer automatically changes the bitmap (.BMP) file that Windows loads as wallpaper—the graphics that make up the top of the Windows desktop—each time it starts up. It makes every time you start your machine a real adventure, especially if you assemble a large collection of interesting wallpapers.

How to Use Wallpaper Randomizer

Wallpaper Randomizer is the only DOS program in this book: We've included it because it is simple to automate in your DOS startup. Lest this offend Windows purists, access to DOS always has to precede launching Windows: Your PC always boots under DOS, even if you never touch the stuff otherwise. Wallpaper Randomizer can easily be installed as a line in your AUTOEXEC.BAT file so that it will randomly select a new wallpaper for you each time DOS starts up, or you can run it as a DOS command line application. Either way, here's how:

C:\>**WALLRAND C:\WINDOWS**

What this command says to the PC is "run the WALLRAND program"—that's the filename for the Wallpaper Randomizer program—"and look in the C:\WINDOWS directory for WIN.INI and any files that end with .BMP." WIN.INI is actually the file that loads Wallpaper when Windows starts up, and .BMP indicates that a file is a bitmap file suitable for use as wallpaper.

To edit your AUTOEXEC.BAT file, you'll need to use Notepad in Windows, or any ASCII text editor from within DOS (for example, EDLIN, EDIT, and so on). Any time you change AUTOEXEC, it's a good idea to make a backup and to initiate changes from a floppy to test them out before changing your runtime environment on your hard drive. Working on a floppy means that you can get back to where you started from just by removing the floppy that's causing problems, and re-booting from the original version on your hard drive. This sounds and is simple, but it is too often overlooked as a failsafe method, even by the professionals (ouch! we know!!).

There are a few, possibly subtle, implications of this command:

- Unless you copy the file WALLRAND.EXE to the C: root-level directory, DOS has to be able to find the file through its PATH definition. If you don't know what this means, copy WALLRAND.EXE to the C: directory. Assuming that you've used the defaults for SWT-INST, the DOS syntax is:

C:\>COPY C:\WINDOWS\WALLRAND\WALLRAND.EXE C:

- If you tell WALLRAND that the directory where WIN.INI and the .BMP files reside is C:\WINDOWS, you'd better be sure that's where they live. If not, the program simply won't work.

  Warning: Running WALLRAND with an improper or incorrect location for WIN.INI will produce all kinds of strange error messages, for example "RUNTIME ERROR 003 at 0000:0039." This is because it fails a file read during the startup process while executing AUTOEXEC.BAT. Likewise, if the bitmap files that Wallrand is supposed to use are not located in C:\WINDOWS, a similarly arcane message

("RUNTIME ERROR 0002 at 0000:019E") will result. The upshot of this hoopla is that you shouldn't use Wallrand unless you adhere to the default Windows and Stupid Windows Tricks installations.

- If you're running a machine in the office or some other public place, you need to be aware that WALLRAND really is random. If you've got any offensive or risqué .BMP files in that directory, it's just a matter of time before they pop up. Discretion demands a judicious collection of .BMP files to randomly select from.

The best way to learn how to use the program is to create a bootable floppy with DOS and your normal AUTOEXEC.BAT and CONFIG.SYS files, and then to edit the AUTOEXEC.BAT file to call WALLRAND. If that works, you can then copy the edited AUTOEXEC.BAT file to your hard drive and proceed; if it doesn't, you can restore normal operations simply by rebooting from the hard disk. It's best not to change critical files like these until you're pretty sure they work correctly, and the floppy method we just outlined is one sure way to stay out of trouble.

For the same reason, it's also a good idea to make a backup copy of the WIN.INI file that Wallpaper Randomizer will edit: If something should go wrong, you'll have a known, good working copy to go back to.

Escaping Wallpaper Randomizer

Since Wallpaper Randomizer runs as a single-line DOS command, there is no escape from any particular execution of the program once it's started (short of rebooting the machine while the command is being processed). If you've installed a call to WALLRAND.EXE as a line in your AUTOEXEC.BAT file, removing that line from the file will cancel further calls to the program; if you've elected to call the program from DOS directly, simply elect to no longer do so and the program will trouble you no further.

Suggestions for Using Wallpaper Randomizer

Since it's a pretty simple-minded program, you can install it in your AUTOEXEC.BAT file and then watch the results each time you start up windows. As a trick on others, it's totally benign, and it should be fun to watch people's reactions as they begin to figure out that their wallpaper keeps changing.

If you're going to use Wallpaper Randomizer, you'll want some new .BMP files to add to the collection that Microsoft includes with Windows. To get you started, we've included two taken from the public domain: REVENGE.BMP and ROACH.BMP. Try them out and see what you think. Wallpaper resources for additional files abound, though, ranging from co-workers to user groups to any of the many bulletin board services out there (see Appendix A for some helpful Windows resources, and check out our order form at the end of the book if you'd like to get some additional graphics from us).

Another Background Diversion

We're going to digress here and talk about an especially devious thing you can do to your desktop—or someone else's—without too much trouble. Windows reads graphics files to create its Wallpaper; the Wallpaper establishes the desktop background on top of which all windows will open. Figure 28 depicts the Control Panel that Windows uses to provide basic system controls, along with the Desktop controls that provide the tools to control your windows and desktop backgrounds.

The Wallpaper selection will be of special interest here because we will use it to play a subtle kind of trick by making a background that looks like an active window. Basically, all you need to do is to make a screen shot of a regular working desktop. This requires a four-step maneuver:

1. Create a normal-looking desktop, perhaps with the File Manager or the Program Manager open to a regular working configuration. Press the Print Screen key (usually marked "Print Screen" or "Prt Sc" on the keytop) to capture the entire screen to the Clipboard, or

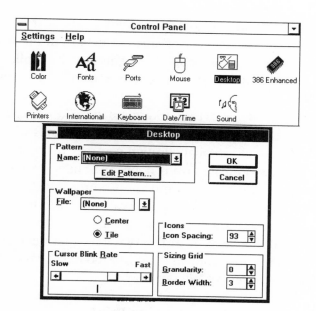

Figure 28: Windows' Desktop controls

use Alt-Print Screen to capture only the currently active window. Either way, you're getting a snapshot of the information needed for the trick.

2. Open the Windows Paintbrush application from the Accessories Program Group (which comes with Windows) and select Paste from the Edit menu. This takes the contents of the Clipboard and pastes it into the Paintbrush application.

3. Select Save As from the File menu in Paintbrush and save the file you've just created into the Windows root directory (usually C:\WINDOWS) under the name DESKTOP.BMP.

4. Exit Paintbrush and start up the Control Panel (in the Main Program Group), selecting the Desktop controls. Select the file named DESKTOP.BMP as your Wallpaper in the Wallpaper section, and make sure that the Center radio button, rather than the Tile button, is on (tiling may cause the file to be reduplicated, giving away the trick).

While the description is somewhat taxing to read, it really doesn't take very long to execute. And because it can be done on virtually any Windows machine—most people leave Paintbrush installed because it comes with Windows—it can be set up in one or two minutes on any Windows desktop.

The trick is that it makes the background look like an active Window and will cause its user to mouse around on pictures of application controls rather than actual application controls. It's pretty benign as tricks go because no real harm is done, and changing the wallpaper simply requires getting back into the Control Panel, selecting the Desktop controls, and changing the Wallpaper selection. We've described this trick here because you can even just capture the DESKTOP.BMP file, leave it in the Windows root directory, and let WALLRAND take over, knowing that DESKTOP.BMP will show up as the wallpaper selected for Windows sooner or later.

Wallpaper Randomizer: The Fine Print

Wallpaper Randomizer is copyrighted software, but it may be freely copied and distributed. The author does not request any donations or payments for its use.

Wallpaper Randomizer 1.0
© 1991
written by Stephen R. Kifer
CompuServe address: 70421,152

Please send any comments or suggestions you might have about the program to Stephen at his CompuServe address, or write him at:

Stephen R. Kifer
205 Hale St.
Macon, MS 39341
Internet address: srk1@Ra.MsState.Edu

Wallpaper Randomizer: The Files

README.TXT	Documentation file for Wallpaper Randomizer
WALLRAND.TXT	Wallpaper Randomizer program
ROACH.BMP	Public-domain bitmap
REVENGE.BMP	Public-domain bitmap

The two bitmap files are not part of Wallpaper Randomizer; we've included them to help you get your .BMP collection going. If you check out our order form at the back of the book, we can also send you entire floppies full of graphics to add (space considerations kept us from adding more to the SWT diskette).

WinRoach

Bugs Ahoy!

What WinRoach Does

WinRoach is an absolutely charming piece of nonutilitarian programming. It sets a herd—or is it a horde?—of roaches loose on your desktop, moving at random to hide behind any open windows or icons that might be nearby. Thereafter, any time an icon gets moved, or a window is opened or closed, these electronic critters will scurry for the nearest cover, just like the real thing! WinRoach keeps a constant flurry of activity on your desktop and helps to make figurative bugs real.

How to Use WinRoach

Firing off WinRoach requires only that the program file be double-clicked in the File Manager, but it is also possible to invoke WinRoach with meaningful parameters from the Run command as well. You can specify the number of roaches from 1 to 9 and their speed in milliseconds (we're not sure what this actually means, except that the program uses a default of 100 and that a speed of 50 seems to provide more realistic roach behavior). Here's the general syntax and an example:

C:\WINDOWS\WINROACH\WINROACH <n> /S <s>
C:\WINDOWS\WINROACH\WINROACH 8 /S 50

<n> indicates the number of roaches, which must be a whole number from 1 to 9; <s> indicates speed, which must be a whole number between 10 and 2,000. Our example, taken from the .DOC file, is more realistic: It creates 8 roaches that move at a realistic speed on the desktop. Figure 29 shows what these brutes look like when they're unleashed in the open.

Figure 29: Roaches on the run!

Once WinRoach gets started up, you are first presented with a screen introducing the products of its creators, New Generations Software. Since it features an 800 number for orders and prominently displays both Visa and MasterCard logos, this was our first clue that we were dealing with a pretty professional outfit. We're glad to say that the software that follows does not disappoint, even if the reminders to register and pay can seem a bit daunting (remember, paying for shareware is what keeps these outfits in business, so I guess we shouldn't blame them).

After you agree to the basic terms of the software license (the button to continue reads "I Agree" rather than the more usual OK), a roach-shaped icon labeled WinRoach hits the desktop. A single click on the icon calls up the control panel. In addition to the usual Windows application controls, we find the following entries:

84

- Add Roach lets you add roaches to your population, up to a maximum of 10, one roach at a time.
- Delete Roach deletes roaches, one at a time.
- Options leads to the basic program controls, as depicted in Figure 30. Here you can set the default number of roaches between 1 and 10; set basic roach speed from slow (high) to fast (low); and establish roach-wander frequency.
- ReScatter redistributes the bugs randomly around the screen so you get to see them scurry for cover!

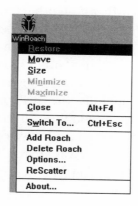

Figure 30: WinRoach controls

In getting familiar with the program, we observed that the defaults work pretty well for the machines we tested on, but you should play with the controls to see what works best for your own desktop. We especially like the newly added Wander capability, which causes the roaches to move about on their own from time to time rather than only when a window is moved, opened, or closed.

One of the nicest touches about WinRoach is that you can squash the little buggers by clicking on them with your mouse. We assume that this is why it's possible to add roaches to the population, but this activity, which produces a nice graphic for a squashed roach, lends a certain gamelike quality to an already interesting program.

85

Escaping WinRoach

Despite clearly anarchistic tendencies, WinRoach behaves admirably within the Windows environment: It can be halted with any of the usual techniques, including a Close command or its Alt-F4 keyboard equivalent through the icon, or ended as a task through the Task List. But we found ourselves having so much fun with the program, we didn't *want* it to stop.

Suggestions for Using WinRoach

Like a couple of the other really stellar tricks in the book, WinRoach deserves a home on your own desktop as much as it does on someone else's. If you do have to inflict it on others, make sure you hide the WinRoach icon: We found that it can be secreted behind the Program Manager icon particularly well because it is nearly a perfect fit. Since WinRoach can be turned off in so many predictable ways, hiding the icon will only slow things down a while, but it should prolong the hunt and, hopefully, the thrill of the chase. No wonder they say that roaches are so ubiquitous in human populations.

Warning: Our testing showed us that WinRoach and Fish! do not get along with each other. If you want to run WinRoach and a screen blanker, we recommend that you try either Fireworks or Magic, but not Fish!

WinRoach: The Fine Print

WinRoach is a product of New Generation Software. The company was formed in early 1991 with the mission of creating innovative graphical software that is fun and easy to use. WinRoach is available for $12.95 for a registration number only, and $17.95 for a mailed diskette with executables and the WinRoach source code (price includes shipping and handling charge). We encourage you to register. They can be contacted at:

New Generation Software
P.O. Box 89042
Houston, TX 77289
(800) 964-7638

Author's Comments

Roaches, roaches, roaches everywhere!!! They scurry across the screen and hide under Windows. Exterminate those PESKY roaches by clicking on them with your mouse! WinRoach is an entertaining game for Microsoft Windows that can provide hours of fun.

Need we say more?

WinRoach: The Files

REGISTER.EXE	Brings up a utility to add your name and registration number to your copy of WinRoach
WINROACH.DOC	Program documentation file; full of worthwhile details about the program and its use
WINROACH.EXE	WinRoach program, please play!

Sounder

DSOUND Control Panel

The PCs are Alive with the Sound of Sounder!

What Sounder Does

Sounder makes it possible for your PC to play digitized sound files, and there are an astonishing number of such files available. Once you get to know this program, your PC will be silent no more. Not only will you be able to hear it repeat famous (or infamous) movie lines, but it will also be able to talk like cartoon characters and much more!

How to Use Sounder

Because playing digitized sounds on the PC's built-in speaker requires the support of a special driver, installing Sounder is a two-step process: First, you have to install a Digitized Sound Control Panel, called DSOUND, which will help you set up your PC to do the best job it can of reproducing those sounds; second, you will then use Sounder to play those sounds back for you.

Installing the DSOUND Control Panel is easy: Double-click on the file named SNDCNTRL.EXE in the C:\WINDOWS\SOUNDS directory and the panel will introduce itself to you. It is also necessary to have the dynamic link library that provides functions to the sound control panel and driver, called DSOUND.DLL, available to both programs. The program's author recommends that this file be moved to C:\WINDOWS\SYSTEM, but we found that it works equally well as long as you keep DSOUND.DLL in the directory where the SWT-INST.BAT program installs it for you.

As depicted in Figure 31, the DSOUND Control Panel provides controls to get your CPU to match the frequencies needed to accurately reproduce digitized sounds. In the example shown, the computer is running in Enhanced mode, so it's necessary to adjust the volume to make the test sound audible enough, and to adjust the Delay value to make your computer sound like a famous cartoon character saying "Aw, come on, I'll cheer ya up" when the Test button gets selected. A larger delay means that the sounds will be correspondingly slowed; a smaller delay means that they are speeded up. You'll need to play with this setting to get sound playback to work on your computer; the settings for Volume and Delay depicted in Figure 31 were those that worked best on our 386SX-16 test machine.

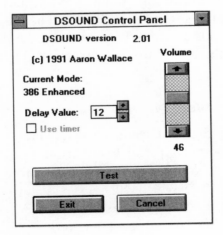

Figure 31: The DSOUND Control Panel

If you're running Windows in either Real or Standard mode, start out by setting the volume to 10 and click on the Use Timer check box. Use the Test button to set your volume correctly. If the sounds emitted are not recognizable as the sound described earlier, you may have to use the Delay feature as with Enhanced mode operation. This will depend primarily on the speed of your CPU—faster chips are more likely to need Delay support to work, while slower ones (10MHz and below) will typically work well with the Timer.

In the background, the DSOUND Control Panel is saving the settings you establish in the WIN.INI file; this happens when you click on the Exit button in the program. Based on the settings that worked best on our 386SX test machine, the entries to WIN.INI looked like this:

[DSOUND]
EDelayValue=12
Volume=76

If you were running in Standard or Real mode and were using a Delay setting, you'd see an entry labeled SDelayValue or RDelayValue instead; if you used the Timer, you'd see a TimerValue. These values can be manually entered into your WIN.INI, but we think it's easier to let the application do it for you.

Once you've established the right settings for the driver, you're ready to play back some sounds. Double-clicking on SOUNDER.EXE won't get you anywhere because it has to have a sound to play back in order to do anything. Instead, we're going to change Windows' ability to recognize that files with .SOU or .SND extensions need to be played back by SOUNDER.EXE, as shown in Figure 32. There are two ways to do this:

- File Manager. By highlighting a file with the .SOU extension and selecting the Associate selection under the File
  menu with the Sounder application, we instruct Windows
  to call Sounder any time a file of that type is double-
  clicked. After you do this, you'll notice that the .SOU files'
  icons in the File Manager change from empty boxes
  (which means that Windows doesn't know what to do
  with them) to boxes filled with small lines (which means
  that Windows has an association to an application established for that file type).

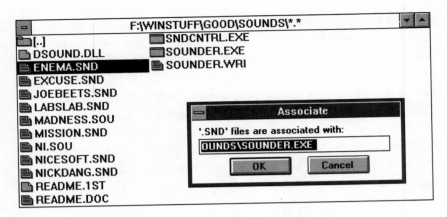

Figure 32: Associating .SND files with SOUNDER.EXE

- The second method is a variation on the first and consists of editing your WIN.INI file to add definitions that instruct Windows to set up these associations for you. From Notepad, or a DOS-based ASCII text editor, look for the section labelled [Extensions] in WIN.INI that includes definitions like:

wri=write.exe ^.wri

This informs Windows that files ending with .WRI should be passed over to WRITE for execution; what we're going to do is add definitions like:

sou=c:\windows\sounds\sounder.exe ^.sou

that tell Windows to pass .SOU files over to Sounder for execution.

If you elect to use this method, make sure to keep a backup of your old WIN.INI file in case you inadvertently change something you shouldn't. You might also want to consider using the floppy boot test method that we described in the chapter on Wallpaper Randomizer to try out your changes.

92

Note: If you use the method described in the preceding section, this step isn't necessary because using the Associate mechanism in the File Manager automatically changes WIN.INI for you. If you do elect to edit WIN.INI, you'll have to exit and reenter Windows in order for any changes to take effect (Windows only looks at WIN.INI as it starts up).

One thing to be aware of when using Sounder is that playing back sounds is a very time-sensitive operation. This means that Sounder interrupts all ongoing Windows processes while it's playing a sound, to make sure that the pitch and intensity are properly controlled. This will halt all other activity while the sound is playing, and will usually result in display of the hourglass cursor at the same time (indicating in this case that input must wait for the sound to finish playing).

Escaping Sounder

Because Sounder runs only while it's playing sounds, there is no real way to escape except by punching Alt-F4 while the sounds are playing. And this may not make a difference. It depends on when Windows notices those keystrokes as opposed to when it plays back the sounds. If you don't want to play any sounds, just don't run any sound files.

If you're running the DSOUND Control Panel, it can be exited through any of the usual methods: Choose Close through the Control button, use Alt-F4 as its hotkey equivalent, or choose End Task through the Task List.

Suggestions for Using Sounder

Sounder is a terrific Windows toy. We recommend that you use it and play with it to your heart's content. It would take considerable ingenuity, however, to get it up and running on somebody else's desktop. First, you'd have to tune the DSOUND Control Panel on their machine for accurate playback. Then, in addition to copying Sounder and the sound files to their machine, you'd have to set up the file associations. But since we know some of you will stop at nothing to get a technological leg up on your colleagues, we're sure that some of you will conspire to find a way to deal with these trifling obstacles. If you must indulge in such childish antics, please remember to trick responsibly (think of it as Safe Computing).

One word of caution: The speakers that most manufacturers put onto PC motherboards leave a lot to be desired in terms of sound quality. In our initial test battery of five machines, only two sounded even halfway decent, while the others were pretty lame. If sound on the PC is important to you, you should strongly consider adding an audio board like the Sound Blaster Pro (recommended by Microsoft for its Multimedia PC configuration).

There are a huge number of digitized files that Sounder can play that are available from a variety of resources. Most BBSs that offer Windows stuff will include them, and you can even order additional diskettes full of such stuff from us (see the order form at the end of the book).

Readers with access to CompuServe can obtain additional sound files from the Advanced Windows User Forum (GO WINADV) and from the Macintosh Fun Forum (GO MACFUN). To use Macintosh sound files with Sounder, they must first be converted from Mac to PC format, which may be accomplished by using a PC program named UNSIT.EXE, also available on MACFUN. We also offer additional diskettes of compressed sound files for your delectation on the order form at the end of this book.

Sounder: The Fine Print

Sounder and the associated programs are copyrighted software offered to the public as shareware and are the work of Aaron Wallace.

Aaron Wallace
P.O. Box 13012
Stanford, CA 94309-3020

Aaron Wallace can also be reached through the internet at aaron @ jessica.stanford.edu. It's also worth investigating some of the friendly front-end programs to Sounder available on CompuServe (GO WINADV or WINNEW), such as PLAYER and SoundTool, which provide a way to link sounds together and to programs, and to record and edit digitized sounds, respectively.

The current shareware registration fee for Sounder 2.01 is $2. At that price, it's the lowest charge for any fee-specific shareware program in this book. If you do use this program, please send him the money. We liked it so much we sent him significantly more than he asked.

Author's Comments

Sounder was my first shareware product, and despite the slow start with Sounder 1.0, Sounder 2.0 has been quite popular. Many thanks to all who registered! Shareware may not be the road to riches, but it is very rewarding to see your program on BBSs across the country and to receive registrations from as far away as Australia and France. I also thank those who have helped distribute Sounder worldwide.

Sounder was a reaction to the Windows 3.0 Control Panel's Sound option: beep or no beep. Not very rewarding, especially when compared to what the Mac users I knew were playing on their machines. Ahh, MacEnvy—Windows needed sound!

I developed Sounder with the hope that others would write Windows programs that supported it. It's not that hard, and sound can make a program much more lively and fun. Since Sounder's first distribution, SoundTool, WinSound, Wired for Sound, BartEyes II, and others have come along. Many thanks as well to the developers of such applications. (Read the SOUNDER.WRI file for information on using Sounder with applications you develop.)

The offer for free upgrades to those who register now still stands, and version 3.0, with support for different sound replay devices, recording, and better programmer support, should be nearing completion by the time this is printed. It'll cost $3.

Sounder: The Files

SOUNDER.EXE	Sound playback program
SOUNDER.WRI	Sounder documentation file (*must* read!)
SNDCNTRL.EXE	DSOUND Control Panel
DSOUND.DLL	Sound resources dynamic link library
DSOUND.LIB	Linkable sound resource object library
DSOUND.H	C constant definitions for DSOUND
BEAM.SOU	"Beam me up, Scotty"
2OTH_CEN.SOU	20th Century-Fox theme
ILLCHEER.SOU	"Aw come on, I'll cheer ya up!"

Appendix A: Windows Resources

Useful Books

Microsoft Corporation: *Microsoft Windows Graphical Environment User's Guide*, Version 3.0, Microsoft Press, Redmond, WA, 1990.

> This is the book that comes with Windows 3.0 and, unlike a lot of other Microsoft product documentation, is well worth reading and rereading.

The LeBlond Group: *Windows 3 Power Tools*, Bantam Computer Books, New York, NY, 1991.

> This book is chock-full of technical information about how Windows works and how to tune your computer to get the most out of the program. At $49.95 (list price), it has to be good to be worth it, and fortunately, it is indeed an excellent resource. If the book has any fault, it's a bad case of technical overkill, but that's what makes it such a good Windows reference. The book also includes a 3.5-inch HD diskette filled with shareware utilities and tools.

Brian Livingston: *Windows 3 Secrets*, IDG Books, San Mateo, CA, 1991.

> Brian Livingston is the president of Windows Consulting, Inc., and writes a regular Windows column for *InfoWorld*. He obviously knows his stuff, and he shares an awful lot of useful information in his recent book. This is probably the single best commercial reference mentioned here.

Ron Person and Karen Rose: *Using Microsoft Windows 3*, 2nd edition, Que Corporation, Carmel, IN, 1990.

> This book is more of the "gentle introduction" sort and is highly recommended for those who may be looking for basic information about how to use a computer and Windows applications, in addition to learning more about Windows and how it works.

Other Resources

Brian Moura (76702,1337): *Windows on CompuServe: A Guide to Windows Vendor Support Areas*, quarterly electronic newsletter.

> Brian is cited several times in this book as a Windows resource in his own right (he also graciously consented to be one of our beta testers). He publishes a revised edition of his resource newsletter quarterly which, despite its title, also covers a broad range of resources outside CompuServe—including Microsoft's own BBSs—as well as in the various CompuServe forums. If you want to go prowling for Windows software, this is *the* tool for the job!

Brian Livingston, "Window Manager"—regular column in *InfoWorld* magazine, IDG Publications, San Mateo, CA.

> Brian is already cited for his excellent book, but we also wanted to refer you to his excellent biweekly column. He regularly covers tips and tricks for tuning or improving your Windows environment, some of which can easily be turned into Stupid Windows Tricks (for example, his October 7, 1991, column "Replace the Windows Start-Up Logo with One of Your Own," could have many tricky applications!).

Appendix B: SWT-INST.BAT Revealed

Introduction

We'll include the full text of the .BAT file here, with additional commentary included in REM (remark) statements. If you're perverse enough to type the whole thing in as is, it should even work! We think you'll find its electronic counterpart—already on the disk that came with the book—much easier to use, but we also wanted to explain what the install program does and how it works, should it become necessary for you to make any changes.

Starting Up the Installation

The key to a successful installation of the Stupid Windows Tricks is changing the system default drive to the floppy drive where you've insert the Stupid Windows Tricks diskette. If this is the A: drive, you'd need to be in DOS (either by itself or through Windows' DOS Command shell) and enter **A:** at the DOS prompt. Please insert the diskette before you do this or DOS will come back with the following response:

Not ready reading Drive A:
Abort, Retry, Fail?

If you should find yourself in this situation, enter **F** to fail and then supply a valid drive letter when DOS comes back to say:

Current drive is no longer valid>

The reason we built the install program this way is to make it possible to install the tricks from any floppy drive letter you want, based on how your particular system is set up (on our test systems, the 3.5-inch floppy drive letter could be any one of A:, B:, D: or E:).

Once you've shifted over to the install drive with the SWT floppy safely ensconced in that drive, simply enter **SWT-INST** at the DOS prompt to install the program to the C: drive within the WINDOWS directory. The rest of the details about how to change this will be explained within the install program itself, so please read on.

SWT-INST.BAT Verbatim

```
@echo off
REM   An @ sign before a line causes it to not be displayed when
REM   interpreted. We use echo off to turn off the screen echo
REM   of commands as they're processed, and the @ sign to keep
REM   the turn-off command from being echoed as well.
echo     S T U P I D   W I N D O W S   T R I C K S
echo              Installation  Program
echo .
echo If you have not supplied a path specification for where the
echo tricks should be installed they will be installed under the
echo C:\WINDOWS directory. The installation program will soon
echo pause and ask you to strike a key to continue. If you have
echo forgotten to supply an alternative directory, or don't want
echo the tricks to be installed under C:\WINDOWS, enter Ctrl-C
echo at the next prompt. This will cause the installation program
echo to halt, and you can elect to terminate it by striking Y in
echo answer to the question "Terminate batch job? (Y/N)"
echo .
REM   We have to put a character (in this case, a period) to keep
REM   echo from telling us if it's on or off after the echo state-
REM   ment. We use a period to denote a blank line throughout the
```

```
REM   .BAT file. All the echo statements with text on them cause
REM   that text to be written to the screen, as we want it to be.
REM
pause
REM   pause stops the batch file from proceeding with the prompt:
REM   Press any key to continue... We use it to stop the screen
REM   from scrolling further, to give the user a chance to read
REM   what's already been displayed.
REM
REM   check for default/explicit
REM     default means to use the values that get supplied by the
REM       install program gets none supplied to it
REM
REM     explicit means to use the values that do get supplied when
REM       the install program gets fired off
cls
REM   cls is the clear screen command for DOS.  It wipes the display
REM   clear and moves the cursor to the upper left-hand corner.
if "%1"=="" goto default
REM   The if tests whether the program's first argument exists or
REM   not, by seeing if it is equal to an empty string, denoted "".
REM   If the string is empty, no values were supplied, so we jump
REM   down to the section labeled :default below; if it is not empty
REM   we continue to the section immediately below, labeled :explicit
REM
:explicit
echo  Parameter-supplied install chosen for %1:\%2. The
echo  Tricks will be installed in a family of directories under the
echo  %1:\%2 directory.  You may enter CTRL-C right now to terminate
echo  this program.
echo .
echo .
pause
cls
REM   The preceding section shows the user who's elected to supply
REM   a drive and directory specification what those values are, as
REM   understood by the install program.  %1 refers to the first
REM   argument fed to the batch file and will be replaced by whatever
REM   the user has supplied (e.g. B or D) and %2 refers to the direc-
REM   tory specification, and will be replaced by whatever the user
REM   had supplied (e.g. TEST or FINALS\SWT).  This is followed by
REM   a pause to give the user time to read—and bail out of—the
```

101

```
REM   choices, and a clear screen to once again clear the display.
echo .
echo Explicit installation requires two arguments:
echo 1. the drive letter where the target directory resides
echo    Do NOT follow the drive letter with a colon (":")
echo 2. the specification for the directory under which the
echo    Stupid Windows Tricks should be placed.
echo    Do NOT precede the directory name with a backslash ("\")
echo .
echo to "trick" the program into moving files under a directory
echo other than WINDOWS, you will have to create a dummy WIN.INI
echo file (because the install program looks for that file name)
echo in the target directory. You can create such a file very
echo quickly within DOS by typing the text within quotes below
echo    "COPY CON WIN.INI"
echo    "TEXT"
echo    " ^ Z"
echo The last character is a Ctrl-Z, and terminates the file entry.
echo By copying this bogus WIN.INI file to wherever it's needed,
echo you can force the install program to work.  It's easier just
echo to put it under your real WINDOWS directory, though.  If you
echo do create a bogus WIN.INI file, DO NOT do so in the WINDOWS
echo directory—you will *DESTROY* your real WIN.INI!!!
echo .
pause
cls
REM   This screenful of information describes how to use an
REM   explicit installation other than WINDOWS (where WIN.INI nor-
REM   mally resides). COPY CON is a DOS command that instructs DOS
REM   to copy whatever you key in at the console (keyboard) into a
REM   named file—in this case, WIN.INI. The Ctrl-Z at the end is
REM   critical, because it's the only way to stop keying into the
REM   file and to get back to the DOS command line.
REM
if not exist %1:\%2\win.ini goto badloc
if not exist stup-win.exe goto badloc
copy stup-win.exe %1:\%2
if not errorlevel==0 goto badloc
%1:
cd %2
stup-win.exe -d
del stup-win.exe
```

```
REM
REM  This is the section of the install program that actually does
REM  all the work.  The first line makes sure that WIN.INI exists
REM  within the target directory (that's how we check to make sure
REM  the directory exists).  The second line makes sure that the
REM  SWT compressed tricks file exists.  The third line actually
REM  does the copy from the floppy to the designated drive and
REM  directory.  If any error is detected, the next line will
REM  catch it.  The %1 line instructs DOS to go to the designated
REM  drive, while the cd %2 line instructs DOS to then change
REM  into the designated target directory.  After this, the com-
REM  pressed tricks file, STUP.WIN.EXE gets unpacked with its
REM  underlying directory structure preserved (that's what -d
REM  means).  Last, we clean up by deleting the compressed tricks
REM  file.
REM
echo  File installed; compressed Tricks file deleted!
echo  To install Tricks, start up Windows and follow instructions
echo  from the book.  ENJOY!!
goto done
REM
REM  This section ends the handling of the explicit parameters
REM  install.  It tells the user it's completed successfully and
REM  then jumps to the end of the install program (:done).
REM
:default
REM  Default install follows
echo You have chosen the default installation.  The Stupid Windows
echo Tricks will be installed in a family of directories under the
echo C:\WINDOWS directory.  You may enter CTRL-C right now to
echo terminate this program.
echo .
echo .
if not exist c:\windows\win.ini goto badloc
if not exist stup-win.exe goto badloc
copy stup-win.exe c:\windows
if not errorlevel==0 goto badloc
c:
cd c:\windows
stup-win.exe -d
del stup-win.exe
REM
```

```
REM  This section exactly parallels the explicit installation
REM  above, except it supplied the target drive (C:) and directory
REM  (WINDOWS) by itself.  Otherwise, all the error-checking and
REM  activity is exactly the same.
REM
echo  Files installed; compressed Tricks file deleted!
echo  To install Tricks, start up Windows and follow instructions
echo  from the book.  ENJOY!!
goto  done
REM
REM  This section ends the handling of the default parameters
REM  install.  It tells the user it's completed successfully and
REM  then jumps to the end of the install program (:done).
REM
:badloc
REM Handle bad location, other errors (WIN.INI not found)
echo  Our install program's error checker failed!  If this is not
echo  because a bad directory reference was supplied, it is because
echo  the install program did not find WIN.INI in this directory.
echo  It needs to find this file in order to work properly; if
echo  you are sure that you want the Stupid Windows Tricks to be
echo  installed into the directory the program has selected, create
echo  a file named WIN.INI in the target directory and the install
echo  will work when you try it again.
REM
REM  This section instructs users as to potential causes of errors.
REM  It is intended to provide guidance about how to proceed with
REM  a successful install on the next try.
REM
:done
REM  This is the last command in the program, and gives the two
REM  install possibilities (explicit and default) a place to jump
REM  to when they've worked successfully.
```

Afterword

Batch file programming is quite an art in DOS and provides lots of opportunities to build useful extensions to your environment. To learn more about programming batch files, we recommend the following books:

> Kris Jamsa, *MS-DOS Batch Files*, 2nd edition, Microsoft Press, Redmond, WA, 1991.
>
> Paul Somerson, *DOS Power Tools: Techniques, Tricks, and Utilities*, Revised for DOS 5.0, 2nd edition, Bantam Computer Books, New York, 1991.
>
> (Somerson has written many editions of this book; for earlier versions of DOS than 5.0, we'd recommend shopping around for an earlier edition at a used book store.)

Glossary

Alt

The way we denote the key labeled Alt on the DOS keyboard; in most applications the Alt key is used to modify the meaning of other keys (that is, it is used in combination with other keys). In Windows, Alt-F4 is used to close most applications, including Windows itself (from the Program Manager).

application (a.k.a. program)

Applications are programs. They run when you double-click their names or use the Run command in the File Manager (for example, to run the program Fireworks, double-click on the file named FIREWORK.EXE in the C:\WINDOWS\EYES subdirectory).

argument

Contrary to normal usage, an argument in the DOS or Windows world refers to a value that is associated with a particular command. For instance, in the Run= section of WIN.INI, you can invoke WinRoach with arguments to control the speed and the number of roaches as follows: Run= C:\WINDOWS\WINROACH\WINROACH 8 /S 50, to start the program with 8 roaches and a speed setting of 50 milliseconds.

ASCII

An abbreviation for American Standard Code for Information Interchange. It was originally defined as a 7-bit code (that is, a string of 7 digits, each either a 0 or a 1). Because 8-bit bytes are common on computers, pure ASCII is commonly encoded as the rightmost 7 places in an 8-bit sequence. Today, 7-bit ASCII is rarely used; now most PC's use **extended ASCII**, an 8-bit character code that contains 256 characters rather than the 128 defined by the original 7-bit version. This permits the addition of graphics and special characters to an otherwise bland alphabetic and numeric (often called alphanumeric) character set.

ASP (Association of Shareware Professionals)

ASP is an industry group of software developers who have combined to establish a set of guidelines for the production, distribution, and sale of shareware. The group is becoming more and more widespread, and offers boilerplate and legal representation for its developers for licensing and sale, offers a registration program and guidelines for shareware vendors, and offers consumers an ombudsman to arbitrate disputes between ASP members and the public. It is an extremely positive force in the shareware business, and very well respected. For more information about ASP or to resolve a dispute, please write: ASP Ombudsman, P.O. Box 5786, Bellevue, WA 98005.

AUTOEXEC.BAT

The file that is automatically executed whenever you start up your computer. It is used to install TSRs, establish the desired default directory, and establish a working environment whenever the computer is started or rebooted. It is the preferred method for using the WALLRAND program to randomize your Windows wallpaper.

backward-compatible

When old software runs in a new environment, for instance, when you run some of the older SWTs, even though you get a warning window, the software still works, even if it was built for an earlier version of Windows. Most reasonable environments are backward-compatible, to allow users continued access to older software.

108

.BAT

A file extension that indicates that a file contains a sequence of DOS commands. If a file named TEST.BAT is executed, it will have the same results as if the commands it contained were entered, one after another, at the DOS keyboard. It offers a simple but useful programming capability to even the most casual of DOS users. We use a file named SWT-INST.BAT to install the Stupid Windows Tricks files for this book.

BBS (Bulletin Board System)

A BBS is a computerized bulletin board that PC users can log into via a telephone connection and a modem. BBSs can be public, like CompuServe or GEnie, or private (as are many of the ones referenced in the SWT authors' documentation files), but in either case, they provide a generally accessible forum for exchange of information, ideas, and a source for public domain and shareware software.

beta software

Software that a company has tested internally that gets released to a limited number of testers or users outside the organization to give it a second round of testing. The theory is that a **beta test** will expose bugs or problems that an internal test cannot, simply because it exposes the software to a wider range of uses and users and because it takes the software out of the sheltered environment in which it was created. People who get involved in a beta test are called **beta testers**.

BIOS (abbreviation for Basic Input/Output System)

The BIOS is a set of routines for accessing memory, disk, or other computer resources that is used by DOS to manage itself and the PC environment; BIOS routines are also available for use in programs that run in a DOS environment.

byte

A byte is 8 bits (which may be either 0 or 1 in value) of data. It is a very common basic unit for storage capacity, speed (in bytes per second), or memory size in computers. 2^{10} equals 1024: This number is called a kilobyte (abbreviated K or KB); 2^{20} equals 1,048,576: This number is called a megabyte (abbreviated MB).

CD

The DOS Change Directory command. It is used to change one's current default directory to another directory specification (for example, if your default directory is D:\TEST and you enter CD C:\WINDOWS\ANNOY, you will then be located in the directory where the ANNOY programs are placed by the SWT-INST.BAT program).

CGA (abbreviation for Color Graphics Adapter)

CGA is a fairly low-resolution type of color display for a PC (usually rated at 640 horizontal by 200 vertical pixels). It was the earliest form of color display developed by IBM for the PC, and while it offered display of a maximum of 16 colors simultaneously, the resolution was so low this option was seldom used. Likewise, CGA's text representation is crude and less readable than more modern display types.

CompuServe

An online information service that is available worldwide and contains a wealth of PC-related information, public domain software, and is also the meeting place for every conceivable variety of PC enthusiast. We found all of the software in this book on CompuServe and recommend it as a source for information, inspiration, and diversion.

controller

A controller is a special kind of PC adapter card, typically used to manage access to a high-speed peripheral like a hard disk.

110

Control or Ctrl

The way we denote the specific key labeled either Ctrl or Control. In most DOS or Windows applications the Control key is used to modify the meaning of other keys (that is, it is used in combination with other keys). For example, Ctrl-Esc is the sequence we use in Windows to access the Task List.

CPU (abbreviation for Central Processing Unit)

The CPU is the brains of a computer: It contains the arithmetic and logical capacity that makes a computer able to perform logical and mathematical computations, along with working space to permit values obtained from memory to be accessed and manipulated.

CRT (abbreviation for Cathode-Ray Tube)

Any display device that uses a glass screen—for example, a TV set—is likely to be built around a CRT. The term is regularly used to generically describe a computer display, irrespective of graphics or color capability.

default directory

In computer jargon, a default is what the computer assumes that you mean when you don't tell it exactly what to do. A default directory tells DOS the first place where you want it to look when you enter commands at the keyboard (the rest of the search hierarchy is supplied by the DOS PATH). In a rare display of common sense, the DOS design team decided that the default directory should be the one that you're currently located within at any given time. Thus, the English equivalent for the term default directory is "the directory you're currently in."

Del or Delete

Denotes the specific key labeled either Del or Delete (in most applications, it deletes the character covered by the cursor). In Windows, we can use it as a keyboard shortcut to confirm the deletion of a file when running the File Manager.

.DLL

A file extension for Dynamic Link Library, a special type of Windows data and resource definition file that provides reusable objects and routines for animation, sound, graphics display, and so on.

.DOC

A common file extension for documentation files in DOS file systems (for example, WINROACH.DOC contains the documentation for the WINROACH.EXE program).

DOS (abbreviation for Disk Operating System)

DOS is the basic program that permits a PC to operate; it runs all the time and establishes the operating environment (also known as the operating system). The earliest PC versions ran from a floppy disk only, hence the name Disk Operating System. Windows takes over the user interface from DOS, but it still relies on DOS for basic functions.

DOS command interpreter

The command interpreter is that part of DOS that is responsible for reading what's being entered at the keyboard. It recognizes valid commands and passes them on to the correct DOS program so that they can be executed; it also recognizes invalid commands and responds with (sometimes cryptic) error messages.

DOS PATH (see PATH)

DOS prompt

The DOS prompt is the characters displayed on the left side of the CRT that indicates that DOS is ready for command input. The DOS prompt can be controlled by the PROMPT command to tell you all kinds of things about where and when you're working (we recommend including the command **PROMPT PG** in your AUTOEXEC.BAT file because then DOS will always display the default directory as a part of the DOS prompt).

By default, the DOS prompt displays only the drive letter and a right angle bracket; for example, C> for any location on the C drive. We find the drive and directory information provided by setting the prompt to PG much more informative.

112

DOS shell

The term shell originated with UNIX and is used to name the command interpreter that accepts keyboard input; in essence, the shell is a program that runs when other programs are not running that permits a user to communicate with the computer. The most common DOS shell is the DOS command interpreter (see above for a definition), but it is possible to alter that interpreter or substitute a different one using the DOS SHELL command (commonly found in the CONFIG.SYS file) to make the desired changes.

ECHO

A DOS command that can be used to control whether or not command input is automatically written to the screen (turned on with the command ECHO ON and turned off with the command ECHO OFF). ECHO can also be used to write messages to the display from inside .BAT files (for example, the command ECHO Hello World! would cause DOS to write Hello World! to the CRT).

EGA (Enhanced Graphics Adapter)

EGA was developed as a refinement of CGA by IBM, partly in response to the success of the Hercules display. Its resolution was increased to 680 × 350, as was the number of pixels used for character display (resulting in sharper, more readable text displays). Likewise, the number of possible colors was increased to 64, with 16 viewable at any one time.

EMM386.EXE

A system definition file that permits an 80386 or higher-numbered Intel CPU to convert extended memory into expanded memory, and provides support for special memory and disk caching drivers under DOS 5.0. In most cases, EMM386.EXE is used on systems where applications need expanded memory support. Otherwise, this system extension should include the NOEMS parameter, especially under Windows.

.EXE

A file extension for DOS or Windows executable files. Most files that end in .EXE—for example, WALLRAND.EXE or WINROACH.EXE—are DOS or Windows applications.

expanded memory (EMS, a.k.a. LIM-EMS)

The specification for the Expanded Memory System (EMS) grew out of the need for large applications to be able to address larger amounts of memory than afforded by a typical DOS environment, which maxes out at 640K. Lotus, because of its 1-2-3 spreadsheet program, Intel, the developer of the 80x86 processor family, and Microsoft, the developer of DOS, got together to define a version of expanded memory called LIM (Lotus-Intel-Microsoft) EMS, that is still used today for 1-2-3 and a number of other applications with large appetites for RAM.

Windows does not use expanded memory, but it can convert expanded memory back to extended in some cases, and can let applications that need EMS support access EMS memory. On older machines, EMS support is typically obtained by purchasing a special EMS memory card, like Intel's AboveBoard memory extender or similar products from other vendors.

extended memory

Extended memory refers to any RAM addressable above the 1 MB upper memory boundary (which is the limit of memory that DOS can directly address, and also served as the upper limit for addressable memory in the earliest PC 8086 and 8088 CPUs). Newer Intel CPUs can address 16 MB of RAM (80286) or up to 4 GB of RAM (80386 and higher-numbered 80x86 processors), but they must access extended memory by changing processing mode from real (where DOS runs) to protected mode (which supports larger address spaces than 640K). For 80286 processors, this is very time-consuming, but for 80386 and higher-numbered processors, accessing extended memory efficiently was designed right into the chip.

forward-compatible

Means that an application written for a newer environment will still run in an older version of the same environment. This seldom happens with software because new environments typically offer features and functions that their older counterparts do not. Unless software is written specifically to exercise only older features of an environment—and no new ones—new software typically does not work on older environments. This is why software written specifically for Windows 3.0 will not work on older 2.x versions.

fractal

A fractal pattern is one that can be mathematically described, and depends on random selection of points or curves applied according to a type of statistical definition that governs such patterns. These patterns tend to be scaled and self-replicating, so that the degree of their irregularity or fragmentation is identical at all scales (that is, the same patterns repeat, no matter what level of magnification is applied to the display of a fractal pattern). The real interest in fractals is that they describe complex patterns in a simple way: Fractal definitions for the shapes of things like a fern's leaf, clouds, and coastlines all appear to work better than any other form of mathematical description, and fractals are widely used in computer graphics and animation to create more realistic-appearing images.

freeware

Software that is given away at no charge. By declaring a program to be freeware, the developer indicates that he or she surrenders his or her financial interest in that program and that it can be freely copied and distributed without recompense to its creator. Several SWTs are freeware and are indicated as such.

gas-plasma display

A gas-plasma display is a type of display that uses a flat panel consisting of two electrically coated glass surfaces enclosing a gas-charged vacuum. The electrical activity caused by charging a specific position on the screen (called a picture element, or pixel) excites the gas at that point, causing it to glow. Gas-plasma displays are compact (but expensive) and are popular in portable computers.

115

GEnie (General Electric Information Services BBS)

GEnie is a public BBS operated worldwide by GEIS. Like CompuServe, it assesses an hourly connect fee for access, and again like CompuServe, provides an electronic meeting place for exchange of information and ideas, and for access to public domain software, shareware, and freeware. Because it offers better access to users outside the US, GEnie is rapidly gaining popularity and acceptance, and is even being used by some major software companies to distribute updates and software fixes to their customer bases.

graphics card (a.k.a. graphics adapter)

A graphics card or adapter is a plug-in card that gets inserted into a PC that has been designed to drive a graphics display device. Specific types of graphics cards mentioned in this book include CGA, EGA, Hercules, and VGA.

GUI (abbreviation for Graphical User Interface)

An environment used to present how a computer system behaves to its user or users. Windows is the GUI that is by far in widest use, but other important GUIs include X-Windows and the Apple Macintosh user interface.

Hercules

Hercules is the name of a company that developed an early type of PC graphics and text display card used to drive a graphics monitor. The name Hercules has become synonymous with "Hercules-compatible" since many companies other than Hercules now make such display cards. The earliest versions supported graphics displays as well as the IBM extended character set only on monochrome displays, but later versions support color as well.

HIMEM.SYS

HIMEM.SYS is a system definition file included with Microsoft's DOS 5.0 that adds memory management capabilities directly to the DOS environment. It is necessary on machines with more than 1 MB of RAM installed to access memory above the 1 MB upper memory boundary. In the past, third party products like

Quarterdeck's QRAM or QEMM386, or Qualitas' 386MAX were required to effectively manage such memory resources. With the inclusion of HIMEM.SYS with DOS 5.0, the need for (and cost of) such products has been significantly reduced.

icon

The name for the small bitmap pictures or symbols used in the Windows environment to identify a program or program group. By double-clicking on a program icon, you can launch its application; by double-clicking on a program group icon, you can get it to expand and show us the program icons for the members of its group.

IDE (abbreviation for Integrated Drive Electronics)

A kind of hard disk drive that has a built-in disk controller (that's why the drive electronics are said to be integrated).

kilobyte

A kilobyte is 2^{10}, or 1024, bytes. This is a common unit of measurement for computer memory and storage and is commonly abbreviated K or KB.

LCD (abbreviation for Liquid Crystal Display)

The most common technology used for flat-screen displays, particularly those found in laptop, notebook, or other portable computers. Although most LCD displays are monochrome, there are a number of companies that offer color LCD displays, albeit very expensive ones ($1,800 and up).

microprocessor

A microprocessor is a single chip, a highly integrated circuit that typically acts as the brains of a microcomputer (see also **CPU**).

MFM (abbreviation for Modified Frequency Modulation)

A technique used for encoding data onto hard disk drives that was common in the late 1970s and early 1980s. Other, more advanced types of data encoding are used today, with their associated disk controller types.

motherboard

A motherboard is the heart and brains of a PC: It contains the central processing unit (CPU) that, for a PC, is a member of Intel's 80x86 microprocessor family. It also typically includes the keyboard interface, the slots into which adapters must be inserted, and some or all of the PC's random-access memory (RAM).

multitasking

A computer's ability to handle multiple activities at more or less the same time by switching very rapidly from one activity to another. This is generally an advantage, especially in Windows, where it's common to have multiple Windows (and activities) going on simultaneously.

option

An option is a type of argument or parameter for a DOS command, usually one that is constrained to have a particular format or a particular value: It represents one choice among several (or many) possible choices, but it is not entirely arbitrary. In the WINROACH program the options for number of roaches, roach speed, and scatter factor represent the only possible arguments that can be used to control that program's behavior.

parameter

A parameter is a value that is associated with a DOS command. It a synonym for the term argument (see its definition for an example of a parameter/argument).

PATH

The term for the file-search order established by the DOS PATH command (usually included in the AUTOEXEC.BAT file). The DOS PATH tells DOS where to look for things if it can't find them in the current default directory (that is, the directory where you are currently located). It can tell DOS to look in multiple directories on multiple drives and is a very handy way to keep all the programs and commands you regularly use accessible no matter what your current directory may happen to be. The total length of the

DOS path is limited to 128 characters; for this reason, many savvy DOS users abbreviate or shorten directory names, since this technique lets them squeeze more references into their PATH statement.

pixel (abbreviation for PICture ELement)

The term used to refer to a single point on a video display screen. It is used to measure display-device resolution, where a higher number of pixels per inch means a higher resolution, which in turn means a higher-quality display.

phosphor

A phosphor is a substance that glows when electrically excited, typically when struck by an electron projected by the coil in a video display device. Both TV and computer screens rely on phophorescence to produce images.

PKZIP

The name of a very useful file compression program written by Phil Katz's PKWare company. It is a program commonly used to decrease the size of files for storage (to fit more on a hard or floppy disk) or for transmission (shorter files take less time to upload or download). This program is highly recommended (see page 11 for ordering information).

public domain

Software is said to be in the public domain when its developer chooses to make it freely available without restrictions on further duplication or use. From a legal standpoint, public domain means that no individual owns it but that some individuals (or agencies) are recognized as its source. Despite the connotation, public domain software is not always free of charge, but any charges associated with it are supposed to be for reproduction and handling rather than as payment for its intrinsic value. Most software whose development is funded by the government is required to be placed in the public domain.

RAM (abbreviation for Random-Access Memory)

RAM is a form of very fast computer storage space where the CPU can read from or write to when executing programs. It provides the information needed to run programs and to supply them with data; it is also the repository for working results from a program's execution. RAM is volatile, that is, when the computer is powered down, its contents disappear. This is why hard and floppy disks are required in PCs (and other computers), since some form of persistent storage is always needed.

reboot

To reboot a computer is to restart it, either by entering a special key sequence (called a "soft boot" in computer jargon because it uses software to restart itself) or by cycling the PC's power off and then back on (called a "hard boot" because it requires the use of hardware—the on/off switch).

ROM (abbreviation for Read-Only Memory)

A type of computer storage where information gets "burned into" particular circuits. It can be read as many times as needed but cannot be changed. ROM is usually slower than RAM, but it is sufficiently faster than hard or floppy disks to warrant its use for regularly reused programs (the PC uses ROM for its startup routines and for its Basic Input Output System).

runtime environment

When a PC goes through its startup procedures and then fires up an application, it builds a set of definitions for things like the DOS PATH, a collection of environment variables, loads device drivers, and in short, sets up a unique environment specific to that machine. The collection of definitions and device drivers, and so on, that make up the PC's capabilities while it's running is called the runtime environment, and it refers to what's supported and available on the desktop at any given moment.

120

screen blanker

A screen blanker is a program that monitors keyboard activity, keeping track of how long it has been idle. Screen blankers take over the computer display after a certain idle period has elapsed, creating purposely random images. If a video display sits idle, displaying the same image a large part of the time (for example, the main Program Manager windows), the image can actually get burned into a computer display over time. Screen blankers prevent this kind of wear by making sure that the screen is kept equally active over its entire surface. For this reason they are very popular pieces of software because most users tend to leave their computers idle but running most of the time.

shareware

Software that may be freely distributed but whose creators normally request that regular or habitual users help to support the programmer by remitting a fee (usually very reasonable). Shareware authors generally retain the copyright to their work and prohibit others from reselling it without their permission. (Of course, we have permission to redistribute all the shareware we've included in this book.) Many of the SWTs in this book are shareware, and we ask yet again that you send your checks or money orders for those programs that you find merit regular use.

single tasking

Means that a computer is limited to doing one thing only at a time; this is generally regarded as a limitation, because it usually means that it is difficult and time-consuming to switch from one activity (for example, a telecommunications program) to another (for example, a spreadsheet application).

SVGA (abbreviation for Super Virtual Graphics Array)

A kind of computer display that offers very high resolution (typically, 1024 × 768) and 256 simultaneous color-display capability. It is a higher-resolution standard, but one that works very much like VGA, that is gaining popularity as a basic desktop color-display standard. We recommend it highly for Windows use.

SWT (abbreviation for Stupid Windows Trick)

SWTs are the subject of this book—we used an abbreviation to make life easier for all of us.

system crash/system hang

A PC is said to have "crashed" or "hung" when it no longer responds to keyboard input. This very often indicates that the executable image of the operating system has become damaged or corrupted (and explains why we call it a system crash or a system hang). The most common cure is to reboot or restart the machine, very often with the "three-fingered salute" used to issue a warm restart command: <Ctrl><Alt><Del>. Sometimes the keyboard will not even respond to this key sequence, at which time a hard reset (cycling the power switch off and on) is the only way to get back into action. Because of the need to manipulate hardware (the on/off switch), this type of crash or hang is sometimes called a "hard crash." After restarting DOS, it will often be necessary to restart Windows (unless you start it automatically from inside your AUTOEXEC.BAT file).

TSR (abbreviation for Terminate and Stay Resident)

A TSR is a kind of program that stays installed within DOS even when it's not in use, ready to be invoked at a single keystroke. TSRs are commonly used for utility programs like notepads, address or phone books, and other utilities that are handy to have instant access to. They are also used to drive devices like printers, tape drives, scanners, and so on, to permit the PC to be used for other things while also communicating with one or more of these devices.

The drivers used to support network access for PCs are also invariably TSRs and since they control the availability of some very important resources, particularly in the workplace where networks are most common, they should not be tampered with except by those knowledgeable enough to correct any problems or failures that might ensue. Because network access is so very important, we recommend that "dirty tricks" be kept to an absolute minimum in a networked environment.

VGA (abbreviation for Virtual Graphics Array)

The VGA name is derived from a special-purpose integrated circuit used in the implementation of most VGA adapter cards. It supports the greatest number of onscreen colors (256) and the highest resolution (640 × 480) of all of the commonly used graphics adapters.

virtual memory

Virtual memory is a technique that lets a computer address more memory than is actually available as RAM on a given machine. In the Windows environment, a special file called a swap file gets set up on the hard disk, which acts as a staging area for programs or environment components that are loaded but not in active use. Virtual memory provides a place to put things that are idle to make more room in physical memory for active processes and environment components. As long as a user can get by without having all components of his or her environment active at any one time, virtual memory can greatly extend the capabilities of any system. The advantages of its use include quicker access to resources and a broader range of capabilities; its disadvantages are an increase in overhead that can slow overall performance and a definite slowdown whenever a context change occurs that forces an inactive portion of the system to be activated, typically by rendering some other component inactive and swapping the deactivated component out to disk while copying in the reactivated component from disk (that's why they call it a swap file!).

VRAM (abbreviation for Video Random-Access Memory)

A special kind of random-access memory used in graphics display equipment. It is usually faster than normal RAM, and it typically can be read from and written to simultaneously (called dual-ported RAM) so that images can be built by the CPU at more or less the same time they're being displayed by the graphics card.

WIN.INI

The Windows initialization file. It gets read every time Windows is started up and is used to define your Windows environment to load and run utilities or background programs. In general it is used to customize your Windows environment to your specific needs. Many of the SWTs will change your WIN.INI file, so it's important to check on and reverse any changes that would add those programs to your desktop in the event that you no longer want to use them.

working directory

The current default directory as established by the AUTOEXEC.BAT command after reboot or startup, or by subsequent CD commands thereafter. It is called the working directory because that is where one is assumed to be working.

X-Windows

A graphical user interface (GUI) developed for use in UNIX environments. While it is about the same age as Microsoft's Windows, it has exercised a considerable influence on Windows—far more so than the other way around.

.ZIP

An extension commonly used to indicate a file that has been compressed using the PKWare PKZIP utility. Such files must be decompressed before they can be used, typically with PKWare's PKUNZIP utility program.

ZIP2EXE

The name of a program in the PKWare compression utilities that converts .ZIP files into self-extracting programs (in other words, it converts .ZIP files to .EXE files—hence the name).

Order Form

Items for Order

We can supply the following items to you if ordered using the included form.

Uncompressed Windows Tricks Diskettes

5.25-inch HD (1.2MB) floppies, decompressed   total: 2

3.5-inch HD (1.44MB) floppies, decompressed   total: 2

3.5-inch DD (720K) floppies, decompressed   total: 3

Windows Sound Files

5.25-inch HD (1.2MB) floppies, compressed   total: 2

3.5-inch HD (1.44MB) floppy, compressed   total: 1

3.5-inch DD (720K) floppies, compressed   total: 2

Windows Graphics Files (Icons, Bitmaps, and so on.)

5.25-inch HD (1.2MB) floppies, compressed   total: 2

3.5-inch HD (1.44MB) floppy, compressed   total: 1

3.5-inch DD (720K) floppies, compressed   total: 2

Each of these sets of diskettes includes either the complete contents of the tricks contained in compressed form as a single 720K 3.5-inch floppy with the book, or a collection of additional sound and graphics files to use with several of the tricks included with the book (there wasn't enough room on the floppy for this extra material). We make them available as a courtesy, not for profit (all fees include shipping, handling, and sales tax where applicable).

We are happy to furnish these copies for you, but they must be prepaid by check or money order. The charge is $5 per diskette (minimum order $10) as indicated below. Orders from outside the United States or Canada, please add $5 for higher shipping and handling costs. Please allow sufficient time for checks to clear if paying by check; money orders will be shipped within seven (7) days.

Please send all orders to:

LANWRIGHTS

5810 Lookout Mountain Dr.

Austin, TX 78731-3618

Order Form

Quantity	Item	Floppies	Total
_____	5.25-inch HD Tricks	2	_____
_____	3.5-inch HD Tricks	1	_____
_____	3.5-inch DD Tricks	2	_____
_____	5.25-inch HD Sounds	2	_____
_____	3.5-inch HD Sounds	1	_____
_____	3.5-inch DD Sounds	2	_____
_____	5.25-inch HD Graphics	2	_____
_____	3.5-inch HD Graphics	1	_____
_____	3.5-inch DD Graphics	2	_____

Total Fee = number of diskettes × $5   Total   _____
(minimum order $10; 1 or 2 disks = $10;
3 or more = $5 × *number* of disks).
Extra handling fee for outside the U.S. and Canada $5.00

Total Fee $ _____

Please remit total fee by check or money order only (no cash, please). Make checks or money orders payable in U.S. dollars to **LANWRIGHTS**. Orders will be processed within seven (7) days of receipt for money orders, within five (5) days after personal or business checks clear. Please fill out the ship-to address below.

Ship to:

Name: _____

Address 1: _____

Address 2: _____

City, State, ZIP: _____